Solution Capsules

Simon Aranonu

WestBow Press books may be ordered through booksellers or by contacting:

WestBow Press
A Division of Thomas Nelson & Zondervan
1663 Liberty Drive
Bloomington, IN 47403
www.westbowpress.com
1 (866) 928-1240

Scripture taken from the King James Version of the Bible.

ISBN: 978-1-9736-7286-9 (sc)
ISBN: 978-1-9736-7287-6 (hc)
ISBN: 978-1-9736-7285-2 (e)

Library of Congress Control Number: 2019912494

Print information available on the last page.

WestBow Press rev. date: 8/23/2019

I dedicate this book to the almighty God and to Ijeoma,
my wonderful wife of twenty-eight years as well as
our children, Dumebi, Naza, Chizzy, and Isaac.

Contents

Acknowledgments

I am grateful to almighty God, who inspired me to write this book. I owe a debt of gratitude to Pastor E. A. Adeboye, the general overseer of the Redeemed Christian Church of God. I am privileged to serve as a pastor in this mission. I am equally grateful to have been sitting under the teachings and tutelage of Pastor Adeboye for the last twenty-five years.

I thank the KRC team, which provided me all kinds of support including free secretarial services for the manuscript. At the top on this list is my friend and boss, Mosun Belo-Olusoga. I will not forget Sr. I.D. Ogufere, Ngozi, Cordelia, Tola, Oluchi, and Toyin. My appreciation goes to Br. Mike A. Maduagwu, my personal assistant, for his prayers.

I appreciate Pastor Sylvester Mbamali for the initial kind review and editing of the first manuscript.

I assure all those who encouraged and supported me on this project that God has at least one solution capsule that will always provide a remedy for any of your challenges.

Preface

A Celebration of Solutions

Life is full of challenges. Believers are not exempt from problems that affect all human beings. Nobody can determine or choose what happens to him or her or decide the timing, shape, or magnitude of some unpleasant events. Challenges can turn up in marriages, families, finances, education, health, fruitfulness, and other areas. Most times, challenges are spiritual though manifest in the physical.

The good news is that every problem has a solution. The irreversible truth is that God's Word contains the solution to all human problems. The joyful news that God wants all humankind to hear is that He has already called us winners and conquerors over all life's problems (Romans 8:37). That is why the Bible says that the One who is inside us is greater than the one who is in the world (1 John 4:4). No wonder Jesus, even as He forewarned us that in the world we would have tribulations, exhorted us to rejoice because He had already overcome the world (John 16:33b). Rejoice now in the light of that gospel truth.

Your celebration starts from the moment it was ordered and guaranteed by the liberating truth in Jesus Christ's eternal word: "You will know the truth and the truth shall make you free" (John 8:32). All the problems confronting you today have solutions in this book, which contains unfailing remedies for any challenges that life brings your way. That is why the book is entitled *Solution Capsules*. You will never again walk alone or be put to shame. Your weeping is over, and your joy commences today (Psalm 30:5). Welcome to your dawn of celebration.

I have had my share of life's struggles. Many times, I was almost overwhelmed by them, and too many times, I despaired as did the apostle Paul. But even in the direst circumstances, the Lord God continually proved His faithfulness to me. It is from those difficult experiences that the chapters of this book were distilled.

As you digest these invaluable capsules, I trust that by the Lord's goodness you will receive your personal solutions. I hope you also start to joyfully witness to your friends, associates, and others that here is a Spirit-inspired manual for victorious living.

I look forward to your personal testimony, and I pray God will bless you very well.

How to Use This Book

Each of this book's ten chapters focuses on a broad area of need including deliverance, healing, restoration, promotion, and others and is divided into sections that dissect a problem described as a challenge.

In the manner of a medical prescription following a proper diagnosis, every challenge set forth in this book is met with a solution by a relevant Word of God that is suitably termed Word Solution. Then follows the Spirit-inspired Prayer Points.

God bless you as you read!

Chapter 1

Deliverance Capsules

Thou Art Loosed

Challenges

- You find yourself moving in circles.
- You feel fettered or bound up.
- You rise and fall repeatedly.
- Your movement in life is at snail speed.

The Word Solution

Many people are bound one way or the other. Some are in prison, some are bound by witches and wizards, and some are handicapped by curses. Some are held down by sicknesses while others are crushed by poverty. Whatever is holding you down is working contrary to God's plan; you are not meant to be held down.

But how would you know that something unseen is holding you down? How would you know whether you are bound by satanic forces? It is not too hard to discern an evil pattern that is alive and working contrary to God's plan for your life. You can tell if you are stagnating or lagging behind your age mates and classmates in spite of your honest, best efforts. Not everybody's destiny is the same, but there is an expectation of progress that should not elude anyone in normal circumstances. If you find yourself too far behind the average, something is fundamentally wrong and slowing you down. It may be an evil influence or an unhelpful burden you need to be loosed from.

If all your age mates are married but contrary to your inner desire you are still single, that go-slow might not be ordinary. If long years into your marriage you still find yourself childless, you need to ask questions of yourself and your Maker because something is wrong. You need to be loosed and set free.

If your schedule for academic or professional advancement has left you behind and all alone at a nameless station, there are pertinent questions you need to ask. If all your fellow tenants have become landlords and you are the odd man out, something may be weighing you down that needs to be addressed with honesty. If a common cure that works for others is not working for you, something needs redress.

Jesus does not like seeing anybody held down in any form by Satan. When He saw the woman with a hunchback, His immediate words were, "Woman thou art loosed" (Luke 13:12). Notice that the woman did not ask to be healed. Notice also that Jesus did not lay hands on her; He only looked at her and spoke to her, and she stood.

The Bible says that Jesus went about doing good and healing all those who were oppressed by the devil (Acts 10:38).

Are you bound today? Ask Jesus to look toward you. He will set you free.

In 1997, I was bound by a nonmedical sickness that threatened my life. It started with an unusual wind that made a swooshing noise at my window one Saturday afternoon when I was lying on my bed wide awake. That wind immediately settled on my stomach in an evil operation that lasted about thirty seconds. From that day, my stomach began to protrude as if I were pregnant. All my dreams became dreams of death. Several of my relations were calling with reports that they saw me dead in their night visions. But God sent Pastor E. A. Adeboye to the town where I was living, and I was privileged to meet him. This general of God laid hands on my shoulders and made a pronouncement: "Father, they will not kill this one."

The following night, I had a dream in which God's angels performed surgery on my stomach and removed a live tortoise. My stomach normalized from that day and became flat again. I am here today still alive and serving God.

The Prayer Solution

- Every judgment keeping me in prison be nullified in Jesus's name.
- Every yoke weighing me down be destroyed in Jesus's name.
- Every burden slowing down my progress loose your grip over me in Jesus's name.
- Every curse against my progress be broken now in Jesus's name.
- Every power holding me down loose me and let me go in Jesus's name.
- Father, increase my speed and let me begin to excel in Jesus's name.
- Father, root out every foundational power blocking my progress in Jesus's name.

Overcoming Household Enemies

Challenges

- Close relatives and friends are envious.
- You are hated or attacked by close relatives.
- You face peer rivalry.

The Word Solution

Every household has an internal enemy. Jesus gathered twelve apostles to His side, and one of them became a household enemy. His name was Judas. He was stealing from the treasury, and he eventually became an informant who sold his Master to outsiders and collaborated with them to have Jesus killed.

There is a saying that the witch inside informs the witch outside about how to attack a family member. The deadliest enemies are household enemies. That is why Jesus said that a man's enemies would be members of his own household (Matthew 10:36). That is also why David lamented that household enemies had almost destroyed him, and he prayed that God would destroy them all (Psalm 55:12–15).

We often make a mistake by thinking our enemies are far away from us. The truth is that our enemies are often very close by. Some are blood relations, close friends, associates, or colleagues at work. Some might even sneak into our churches trying to win our trust. Joseph's brothers were household enemies who conspired to kill him before deciding to sell him into slavery (Genesis 37:12–36).

Envy is the major driving force behind household enmity. When you achieve success, expect your household enemies to increase. A close relation of mine once challenged contractors I had hired to build my country home. He was unable to contain or mask his envy. He asked the contractors who had given them permission to build such a nice house in the village. He was quoted as saying that I was building a house that would dwarf his house so that I could look into his compound from mine. He then boasted that he would not be alive and see the house completed. To God be the glory that in His amazing love, He kept him alive and the house was completed.

The greatest weapon your household enemies have is their closeness to you and their ability to mask their intentions. You need God's gift of discerning of spirits to be able to know this. You must not let your guard down. The Bible says the devil can operate as an angel of light (2 Corinthians 11:14).

Stop looking far outside for the source or cause of your problems. Look inward. Those who do not know you will not harm you; they have neither motive nor motivation to harm you, but those who know you could become jealous of your progress and want to stop you.

I pray God will open your eyes today and expose your real enemies to you. Pray that God will disappoint their devices. You will overcome in Jesus's name.

The Prayer Solution

- All evil alliances and spy networks working for the enemy in my family, Father, expose and frustrate in Jesus's name.
- Every enemy pretending friendship to me, Father, expose in Jesus's name.
- Every agent of the devil in my family or business circle, Father, expose in Jesus's name.

- Every planting that is not of God in my life, family, or church, Father, uproot in Jesus's name.
- Father, render useless every weapon formed against me in Jesus's name.
- Father, grant me your spirit and wisdom to discern hate and enmity behind the pretensions of people close to me in Jesus's name.

Let There Be Light

Challenges

- You are confused.
- You need divine direction.
- Things around you appear disorganized.
- Evil spirits and evil powers seem to reign in your family.
- Sickness, pain, death, or sorrow seem to pervade your life.

The Word Solution

Darkness is the opposite of light, but it often precedes light. "Let there be light," God ordered at the beginning of creation (Genesis 1:3) at a time of absolute darkness and chaos upon the face of the earth. Light and darkness cannot coexist; one must give way to the other.

Darkness is virtually coterminous with the works of the devil. Most evil things happen under the cover of darkness. It is Satan's comfort zone, place of abode, and mission field wherein his triple assault—to steal, kill, and destroy—is launched against humankind. The Bible refers to a certain category of demons as "rulers of the darkness of this world" (Ephesians 6:12). Because darkness is the abode of Satan, evil activities thrive in darkness; adultery, robbery, murder, and idolatrous practices are examples. Diseases, failure, frustration, violence, poverty, and all such evil circumstances are bedfellows of darkness.

So when God said, "Let there be light" (Genesis 1:3), He meant, "Let the reign of evil cease and let goodness and mercy take over." God decreed that prosperity and good health should take over, that promotion should occur over, that confusion must cease, and that orderliness must take over. It means to let demons and witches cease to reign and to let God and His people reign.

The Bible says that Jesus is the "Light of the world" (John 8:12). It also recognizes Jesus as the Word of God who became flesh (John 1:1, 14). The Bible is the revealed Word of God; when we study it, we are studying Jesus, the Word of God and the Light of the world. Jesus can illuminate our minds and environments spiritually and physically.

In 2005, I met a woman who was a new convert keen to learn the Word of God. She and I studied the scriptures on the balcony of my hotel room for over two hours one evening. I wish you had seen the glow on her face as she ingested the written Word of God precept by precept. The sun was setting, and she was preparing to leave when a strong light shone all over the hotel. She called my attention to it, and we looked up. It was the moon shining seemingly more brightly than the sun. In that opportune light, we were able to continue our Bible study for another two or three hours. She kept reminding me that the moon had not been as bright the previous night, yet it was there for us that night full and bright and shining all night. The following night, the moon did not appear. God had shown proof that He can do anything. He is the Light of the world.

When God said, "Let there be light," He practically meant, "Let Jesus manifest." That is why Jesus showed up in the world. He became man and dwelled among us (John 1:14).

Prophesying the birth of Jesus, Isaiah said, "The people that walked in darkness have seen a great light" (Isaiah 9:2). This Old Testament prophecy was fulfilled in Jesus (Matthew 4:16–17). The light of Christ shines in darkness, but darkness does not comprehend it (John 1:5).

Ask God to shine as light in your family and on all your undertakings. God's light has power to drive all darkness away.

The Prayer Solution

- Every form of darkness in my life, Father, remove in Jesus's name.
- Father, let your light shine continuously in my family in Jesus's name.
- Father, let your light shine on my nation in Jesus's name.

- Father, make me a light to the nations of the world in Jesus's name.
- Every ruler of darkness in my life be dethroned and cast out forever in Jesus's name.
- Let there be light now shining on my destiny in Jesus's name.
- Any evil cloud blocking the light in my life be removed now in Jesus's name.

The Power of Altars

Challenges

- When enemies set up evil altars to attack you.
- When you experience sustained and protracted satanic attacks.
- When enemies consult mediums and false prophets to afflict you.
- When you face recurring problems.
- When you desire accelerated answers to your prayers.

The Word Solution

Altars are meeting points between man and spirits. Evil spirits congregate at evil altars in the same way good altars draw God's mighty power down for communion with humanity. Altars have powers; they are fellowship points.

Evil altars are set up by idol worshippers and may be found in the open in pagan communities, groves, shrines, village squares, markets, and other meeting places. In the more urban cultures of the present day, they are secretly kept by many in the privacy of bedrooms and other hidden places.

Setting up an evil altar is idol worship. God detests evil altars and prescribes their pulling down by His faithful servants. God told Gideon to destroy Baal's altars (Judges 6:25–27). Elijah threw down Baal's altars and had the prophets that ministered to those altars slain (1 Kings 18:40).

Everywhere you find evil altars, there never is progress and social good for the people. Families, villages, and towns that worship idols wallow in poverty and backwardness. They are plagued by frequent calamities and inexplicable afflictions. Young men die in their prime leaving scores of suffering widows and orphans destitute. The nation of Israel fell into such straits when its people worshipped Baal. A terrible drought befell the land in the time of Elijah due to the widespread idol worship under King Ahab and his wife, Jezebel. During an earlier era in the Israelites' worship of Baal, God caused the Midianites to plunder their harvest, and they were forced to live in caves (Judges 6:1–4).

Take a close look at your life, family, and village. Are you still worshipping any idol? Have you sought or made money from an idol or obtained any sort of imagined power or advantage from an evil altar? Disconnect yourself from every evil altar today, and renounce every gain associated with it. Even if your link with an evil altar is a carryover from your parents or other forebears, it is still a curse that is actively hindering your progress today. God has made it clear that He will punish up to four generations for idolatry (Deuteronomy 5:9). Quit stumbling along; break any inherited evil covenant and be free.

I know a rural community that had remained stagnant for years while all its neighbors were developing fast. Their young men were dying off at an alarming rate; their hapless estates were filled with uncompleted projects. The community rose as one and renounced its idols. The picture changed immediately thereafter, and development became the new face of the community.

As you destroy evil altars, set up an altar for the God of Israel in the name of His only begotten Son, our Lord and Savior, Jesus the Christ.

The Bible has a great example in Noah. Right after the great flood that wiped away the entire human race, Noah had a God-assigned responsibility to replenish the earth with all life forms that were saved along with him. He knew that communications between humanity and God had broken down when humankind allowed the devil to come between it and God, their Creator.

The first thing Noah did was to build an altar for God (Genesis 8:20) and offer animal sacrifice to God. The Bible tells us that God smelled the sweet savor of his sacrifice and promised humankind that He would never again destroy the world by water. He also said that seed time and harvest time would never cease from the face of the earth.

Notice again in Genesis 12:7 that the first thing Abram did when

God called him was to build an altar. An altar of God is a consecrated place where God speaks to His elect. If a holy man mounts a true altar of God, his subsequent utterances are invariably prefaced by, "Thus says the Lord." An altar of God is also a place of sacrifice. The best place to offer a gift to God is on His altar. God savors it immediately; worshippers whose hearts are pure make Him happy.

Jesus had a word about purity of heart as a precondition for an acceptable offering to God. He adjured whosoever was bringing an offering to the altar to first examine his heart; if he found in it any trace of bitterness against a brother, he was to lay aside his offering and become reconciled with that brother before returning to offer the sacrifice. An offering cannot be acceptable to God if the giver's heart is not acceptable to Him. An altar of God is a place of constant communication between God and those with pure hearts. Because God is always at His altar, petitions presented on it receive speedy attention that could be even further accelerated if backed by sacrificial offerings.

Do you have a difficult problem that appears to defy solution? Are you facing a challenge that you have prayed and fasted about or even sought counseling and intercession from some men of God for but to no avail? Have you considered taking a sacrificial offering to the altar of God concerning that problem? Be sure to make that offering truly sacrificial, and make sure you take it to a holy altar. Tell God why you are approaching His altar. You are close to your triumphal testimony as God never fails.

I see you rising again. You will still make it. This time, you will not fall.

The Prayer Solution

- Every evil altar raised up in my family be broken beyond repair in Jesus's name.
- Every evil priest ministering at an evil altar within or against my family be removed in Jesus's name.
- Any power, financing, or promoting an evil altar in my family be broken in Jesus's name.
- Any curse of evil altars upon my life be broken now in Jesus's name.

- Every satanic arrangement in my family be dismantled in Jesus's name.
- Every calamity, setback, and defeat I have suffered because of evil altars be reversed in Jesus's name.
- I renounce and disconnect myself from any evil altar ever raised by my parents and ancestors in Jesus's name.

Freedom for Prisoners

Challenges

- When you feel you are going in circles.
- When you dream about being arrested, tried, and sentenced.
- When you are repeatedly rising but then falling.
- When good things meant for you never get to you.
- When you are stagnant in life.
- When in dreams you get locked up.

The Word Solution

It may shock you to learn that many people clapping their hands in ostensible happiness have spiritual handcuffs on their hands. It may amaze you to learn that many who seem to be wearing beautiful garments are actually dressed spiritually in mean prison clothes. If that sounds like a fairy tale, please ask God to open your eyes.

There are many signs to know when someone is in a spiritual prison. A pattern of repeated rising and falling in careers, business, family, and other worthy pursuits is most often not just happenstance. An intelligent, hardworking man could remain impoverished if he is bound in spiritual chains. Another sign of spiritual imprisonment is the almost-there syndrome, a pattern of always failing at the very brink of success.

If you have been going around in circles for a long time, you may have been locked up in a spiritual prison. What is the solution capsule for your deliverance and escape from prison? The psalmist sang, "The snare is broken and my soul is escaped" (Psalm 124:7) and "The LORD looseth the prisoners" (Psalm 146:7). One major reason Jesus came into the world was to set the prisoners free (Luke 4:18).

Every one of us needs divine intervention in this world of sin and spiritual wickedness. Thank God for Jesus, the only one who can set us free. Praise God this moment. Pray for yourself, and ask others to pray for you. Paul and Silas, in chains and in prison, praised God in spite of their dreadful conditions, and God set them free (Acts 16:25). In a related episode, the apostles prayed for Peter while he was in prison, and he was released (Acts 12:5–11).

You too can come out of any prison be it physical or spiritual. I see you free already. Rise, cry out to God, and praise Him.

The Prayer Solution

- Father, open my spiritual eyes to know who I am before you in Jesus's name.
- Every judgment of Satan against me be nullified now in Jesus's name.
- Every false accusation against me or my family be canceled in Jesus's name.
- All those conspiring to lock me up be scattered like chaff in Jesus's name.
- I tell any house of bondage baiting or awaiting my soul that the snare is broken and my soul has escaped in Jesus's name.
- Every satanic judgment against my soul be annulled in Jesus's name.
- As the son of God has set me free, any enemy attempt to lock up my destiny will fail in Jesus's name.

The Lord Will Fight for You

Challenges

- When you keep fighting and losing.
- When your enemies are too strong for you.

- When there is an evil gang fighting you.
- When the battle is still raging and you have exhausted all your weapons.
- When you want the Lord of Hosts to deal with your enemies.

The Word Solution

A friend once asked me, "When will all these battles end?" I laughed because I knew the battles would not end until we got to heaven. I knew also that as soldiers, we were meant to fight battles. I knew as well that the kingdom of heaven suffers violence and that only the violent can take it by force. One basic truth no believer should ever forget is that our adversary the devil is like a roaring lion moving about looking for whom to devour.

In the three years of His earthly ministry, Jesus, our Master, fought hard battles. He warned us to expect the hate and persecution from the world that He had suffered (John 15:20). But being human, we are flesh and cannot fight nonstop. We need intervals of sleep, rest, and recreation. We need to work, and we need to enjoy life with friends and family. I found this was the underlying reason for God's abiding promise that He would fight for us and we would hold our peace (Exodus 14:14). King David, a wise man, asked God to fight against those who fought against him (Psalm 35:1). God advised us to bring our burdens to Him and He would give us rest (Matthew 11:28).

Years ago, a colleague accused me of something I had not done or had ever thought of doing. That accusation caused me so much pain in my heart that I cried all night. But God spoke to my heart that all was well. That was a quiet reassurance to my spirit, and it wiped away my tears even though I was still hurting very much. When God rose on my behalf, the fellow ran into multiple problems only to later confess that someone had asked me to frame him. God fought for me, and He will fight for you.

We need to learn from King Hezekiah, who refused to be drawn into a physical fight with his enemies in spite of extreme provocation. He simply reported them to God, who sent an angel to deal with them on his behalf (Isaiah 37:14–20).

Now that you understand this, go to battle against evil with wisdom; seek divine guidance in prayer and in meditative study of the Bible.

One of God's most unforgettable promises in the Bible is that if we pray according to His will, He will answer us. It is not based on the multitude of our prayers that God answers our petitions; one spirit-filled prayer is more beneficial than a thousand prayers induced by the flesh. The frequency or length of vigils will not solve our challenges; we must live and walk in the Spirit. We who worship God must do so in Spirit and in truth (John 4:24).

Take the right capsule and let God fight for you. Hand your battles over to Him. He knows your enemies and their weaknesses. He has the right weapons, and He cannot lose any battle. He wants to fight for you so you will have peace. Hand over all your battles to God.

The Prayer Solution

- Father, take away my afflictions and give me rest in Jesus's name.
- Relieve me of evil burden, O Father, I pray in Jesus's name.
- Father, fight against those who are fighting me I pray in Jesus's name.
- Every battle over my destiny, Father, I hand over to you in Jesus's name.
- Father, I am laboring too much. Relieve me of vain labor and grant me favor in Jesus's name.
- Father, as you fought for Joseph and David, fight for me in Jesus's name.
- Every Pharaoh determined to destroy me, Father, deal with in Jesus's name.

Deliverance from Evil

Challenges

- When you want to be delivered from your problems.
- When you desire freedom from captivity.
- When you are faced with violent enemies.
- When you suffer inexplicable afflictions.
- When you experience satanic violence.

The Word Solution

In Psalm 14:1, David said, "Deliver me O Lord from the evil man; preserve me from the violent man." My friend, the world is full of spiritual wickedness wrought or ordered by Satan through his human agents. Satan is real as anyone can see or feel in his destructive works. Jesus called him the father of lies (John 8:44) because he uses just about any mean trick he can invent to deceive people.

Violence, oppression, murder, stealing, and destruction pervade the whole earth from age to age. These are the footprints of Satan, who takes joy in stealing, killing, and destroying (John 10:10). But Jesus our Lord suffered crucifixion on Calvary and thereby released the grace of salvation to all humankind through faith. Salvation is deliverance from the works of Satan, the strongman whose only language is violence. The church of Christ can minister deliverance by prayer to God to intervene and save us and ours from Satan's wickedness. As members of the living church, we can secure deliverance by asking God to frustrate the devices of the wicked.

David prayed, "Grant not, O Lord, the desires of the wicked, further not his wicked devices" (Psalm 140:8). The wicked one is always devising strategies to attack us, our dear ones, and every good thing God gave us. We should make no mistake about it—he hates us because we are humans, God's prime creation whom Jesus Christ died for. Satan's hatred gets even worse when by faith in Christ we receive power to become sons of God like Christ Himself. Jesus said Satan and his cohorts would hate us because they hated Him (John 15:20).

In seeking deliverance, we must apply godly wisdom, strictly obey the Word of God, and take nothing for granted. Conventional soldiers will tell you that a basic strategy of warfare is to know your enemy. Can you recognize the enemy? The Bible warns us that the devil can and does masquerade as an angel of light. His aim of course is to evade detection as the enemy he is; he tries to sucker the unsuspecting into a poisoned dinner at his table of death. Samson allied with an enemy positioned against him by Satan and ended up badly. I pray you will not do the same.

Not everybody loves you. The more successful you become, the more Satan will fight your progress by positioning enemies known and unknown against you. Be careful and alert; as the Bible puts it, be sober because your enemy is a roaring lion looking for whom to devour (1 Peter 5:8).

The good news is that God has made a complete provision for your total deliverance. In a dire situation comparable to yours, David cried out to God for deliverance. You need to do so today in total reliance on the Word of God: "Call upon me in the day of trouble, I will deliver you" (Psalm 50:15). God's gracious promise is that when the wicked plot against you, they will be broken in pieces (Isaiah 8:8–10). Do you know that God is willing and able to contend with all that contends with you? (Isaiah 41:10–13). Are you aware that God is ready to take captive all those who want to take you captive? (Revelation 13:10).

Do not remain bound anymore. Stop complaining and murmuring, and behave like King David. Cry out now to God. Do not allow your business to be held captive by evil forces. Do not allow your marriage to be messed up. When God rises, your enemies will scatter (Psalm 68:1). God is waiting for your cry. When the Israelites cried in their bondage, God heard them and delivered them (Exodus 2:23–24).

Your freedom is now as you cry out to God in prayer.

The Prayer Solution

- Father, disconnect me from all evil men and evil associations in Jesus's name.
- Is there an evil man or woman pretending goodness to me? Father, expose them in Jesus's name.
- Father, restrain the violent man from destroying me in Jesus's name.
- Every evil weapon of man programmed into my family, Father, render ineffective in Jesus's name.
- Father, frustrate the strategies and devices the wicked has designed against me in Jesus's name.
- Father, help me be sober and vigilant to discern my enemies in Jesus's name.
- Father, contend with any evil person contending against my life in Jesus's name.

Angelic Warfare

Challenges

- When there is delay in answering your prayers.
- When you desire God's angels to fight for you.
- When the battle is so fierce that you feel outnumbered.

The Word Solution

Before God created human beings, He created angels meant to serve Him and humankind. They worship God nonstop (Revelation 7:11). Yet the Bible refers to them as ministering spirits positioned to serve those who will be saved (Hebrews 1:14). Worshippers of Satan thrive on exploiting the power humanity has over angels. Basically, witchcraft and other occult practices are based on summoning and deploying fallen angels for ungodly assignments. These accursed beings otherwise known as demons are induced by sacrifices offered on evil altars by depraved men and women. Such sacrifices enable Satan's devotees to summon the demons to evil errands against morally upright people, the children of God. The demons obey such summons without argument.

But the good news is that God's angels are always available to act in defense and on behalf of born-again believers. When you pray to God, the Lord of Hosts, He will send His mighty angels to intervene on your behalf. Bible-believing Christians must not pray to the angels or invoke their help directly. Their prayer, warfare, and other assistance must be requested through God, who as the sole owner of the universe may decide to command His angels to go to war on your behalf. For example, when an evil angel, the prince of Persia, battled to delay Daniel's miracles, God sent a good angel, Michael, to overcome that evil contender (Daniel 10:13). In the meantime, Daniel did not let up on his prayer; he kept at it until he saw the full result.

In a similar vein, when God decided to deal with the arrogant Assyrian king Sennacherib, who was tormenting Judah, He sent a single angel to kill 185,000 soldiers of the Assyrian army (Isaiah 37:36). God is faithful to His covenant children and will never be late to act.

Consider what happened when it was time for Jesus to resurrect after three days and three nights after His death and burial; God sent an angel to remove the stone that covered the sepulcher (Matthew 28:2). In much the same way, God needed just one angel to open the prison doors and set the jailed apostles free (Acts 5:19, 12:7). No wonder the psalmist said that God had given His angels charge to protect us against hurt (Psalm 91:11).

In my early years as a Christian, I used to be terrified at night. I had scary dreams, and several unusual physical manifestations occurred in my home. I was living alone in a haunted house. Then one night in a dream, God opened my eyes and I saw angels for the first time—one whose shift had ended and another whose shift had just begun. God allowed me to overhear their discussions. The incoming angel asked the outgoing one for the situation report. His mate assured him that the area was safe and that he had little or nothing to do.

I woke up and remembered Psalm 91:11, in which God promised to give His angels charge over us. I stopped being afraid from that day on as it dawned on me that I was never alone. My friend, there is at least one angel on guard over you.

It is time for you to know how useful God's angels can be to you in spiritual warfare. They are waiting to carry out some great assignments for you, but as ministering spirits (Hebrews 1:14), they can act only on God's instruction, and God will give them instructions concerning you only in response to your prayers. God will not instruct them if you do not engage in warfare prayer or cry in the place of prayer. If Satan has disorganized or destroyed anything in your life, you can cry to God and He will send angels to work for you. If something has been stolen from you, God's angels can see to its timely restoration if you pray for that.

At a recent night vigil, God opened the eyes of a brother to see a casket and some demons in the sitting room. Command was given that the casket be taken away and burned, whereupon almost immediately a second vision occurred in which as commanded, the casket was instantly taken far away and burned.

Start engaging in spiritual warfare and see angels working on your behalf. David petitioned God to let the angel of the Lord chase his enemies (Psalm 35:5). Do the same today to ignite angelic warfare on your behalf. I see angels fighting for you and facilitating your victory for God's glory.

The Prayer Solution

- Father, dispatch your angels to guard my feet against any stone in Jesus's name.
- I command every demon dispatched against me to return to your sender in Jesus's name.
- I renounce any evil angel claiming to be married to me in Jesus's name.
- Every stumbling block hindering my progress, Father, let your angels remove in Jesus's name.
- Let the angels of God proceed now to recover my blessings in Jesus's name.
- Whatever demons on evil assignment in my family, Father, let your angels chase out in Jesus's name.
- Whatever evil spirits have disorganized in my life let the angels of God reorganize and repair in Jesus's name.

The Lord of Hosts

Challenges

- When you need to surrender your battles to God.
- When you need to hand over your labors to God for rest in return.
- When you feel overwhelmed by enemy forces.

The Word Solution

Very often, we want to avenge ourselves on our enemies. But the Lord says vengeance belongs to Him alone (Romans 12:19).

Quite often in our battles, we rely on our human connections and on the physical weapons in our human arsenal. The truth, however, is that our human weapons cannot give us victory because according to the scriptures, our weapons of warfare are not carnal (2 Corinthians 10:4). No matter our private impressions or view on the matter, no human being is our real enemy The Bible makes it clear that our adversary is the devil (1 Peter 5:8).

Any war we wage against a wrong enemy is a lost cause from the start. Wrong or inappropriate weapons employed result in defeat. We fight by ourselves and thus become easily exhausted. No victory is possible when we battle in the flesh in a war that is meant for battling in the spirit. The only way we can win a spiritual battle is by handing it over to the Lord of Hosts. David declared to Goliath, "The battle is the Lord's and He will give you into our hands" (1 Samuel 17:47). Hear again the words of Moses as the Israelites were hemmed against the Red Sea by Pharaoh's pursuing chariots: "The Lord shall fight for you and you will hold your peace" (Exodus 14:14).

In another greatly trying moment, the three combined and intimidating forces of Mount Seir, Ammon, and Moab surrounded Judah to destroy it. But God spoke to His people through a prophet saying, "Ye shall not need to fight in this battle: set yourselves, stand ye still, and see the salvation of the Lord with you" (2 Chronicles 20:17).

Stop struggling to fight all your battles by yourself. Hand the matter over to the Lord of Hosts, who is waiting for your consent to take over your battles. He has never lost a battle because none can battle against the Lord. Let Him fight for you, and you will have your rest.

The Prayer Solution

- Father, please take over all my battles and fight for me in Jesus's name.
- Father, avenge me of my adversaries in Jesus's name.
- At my human limits, O Father, take over and finish every assignment on my behalf in Jesus's name.
- Father, equip me to fight the battles of life in Jesus's name.
- Satan, take your dirty hands off my life in Jesus's name.
- Every problem or challenge in my destiny, Father, I hand over to you in Jesus's name.
- Father, as you did for King Solomon, give me rest from every battle in Jesus's name.

Let My People Go

Challenges

- When you are in desperate need of freedom.
- When you need God's signs and wonders for victory over your enemies.
- When you desire deliverance from oppression.
- When you want the bands of bondage broken.
- When you desire God to silence wicked and stubborn enemies.
- When you are tired of living like a slave.

The Word Solution

For 430 years, the Israelites lived in Egypt. Joseph was their forerunner in his amazing life story that saw him rise from a lowly place as a foreigner and slave to a palatial appointment as prime minister. Joseph brought his father's entire household to Egypt, the land of his highly successful sojourn, thereby saving them from the famine that was ravaging the whole world at that time. But years after the death of both the patriarch Jacob and the favored Joseph, a pharaoh arose who did not know the epic role that the late Joseph had played in saving Egypt. As a consequence, the persecution and bondage of the Hebrews became state policy in Egypt.

If the Israelites suffered in silence at the initial stage of their oppression, they soon began to cry out to God as the torment increased. The Bible records that God heard their cries and raised Moses to deliver them. God's unequivocal mandate to Moses was to go to Pharaoh and demand of Egypt, "Let my people go, that they might serve me" (Exodus 5:1). But Israel's deliverance would not happen without a battle. Pharaoh would put up stiff resistance, but God had His way by enabling Moses to exercise formidable powers and bring Egypt to submission.

Notice that God referred to the Israelites as His people. Take note too that God intervened only when His people cried out. One other point of great significance in the narrative is God's express purpose for delivering His captive people—that they serve Him and not other gods.

God granted His people a special privilege, recompense for their years of misery, pain, and slavery in the land of bondage. He allowed them to spoil the Egyptians as a mark of divine favor; that is evidence that deliverance and divine restoration go hand in hand.

God's eternal desire is to execute uncommon deliverance for all His people. Anyone in bondage can be set free together with his family. Any power that attempts to resist or hinder God's move to deliver someone is asking for special punishment from God.

You will recover all you have lost because God will grant you a special favor as a mark of compensation. But you must make up your mind to serve God and God alone. Get ready for total deliverance, and cry out to God for help; you will have freedom at last from bondage and affliction.

The Prayer Solution

- Every long outstanding problem in my life, Father, please intervene and terminate in Jesus's name.
- Father, deliver me from any sort of bondage in Jesus's name.
- Every ancestral curse or covenant keeping me in bondage, I break and renounce now in Jesus's name.
- From every stubborn spirit fighting against my freedom, Father, rescue me in Jesus's name.
- Father, decree my total deliverance from bondage in Jesus's name.
- Any spirit attempting to lead me into captivity, Father, take captive in Jesus's name.
- Father, as you deliver me and my family from oppression, allow us to recover all that the enemy has stolen from us in Jesus's name.

God of Vengeance

Challenges

- When you are feeling bruised and tired of enemy arrows.
- When you want justice against your enemies.
- When you want an end to sustained enemy attacks.
- When you want God to teach your enemies a lesson.

- When you want God's vengeance on your enemies.
- When you want God to turn the enemy against himself.

The Word Solution

The Bible says it is a righteous thing for God to recompense tribulation to those who trouble us for our faith (2 Thessalonians 1:6). Certain people trouble us and are determined to cause us pain and affliction. The more we show them love, the more they attack and want to maim us and our children sparing no weapon in their satanic armory. They attack us at home, work—everywhere—monitoring us year after year to afflict us more and more. Those are the committed servants of Satan. God knows how and when to punish them with problems they cannot solve, problems that keep them so busy that we get respite.

Ecclesiastes 10:8 says that he who digs a pit will himself fall into it. Psalm 109:17 says because the enemy loves cursing, he too will be cursed. God hates stubborn enemies who will not let you go in freedom to serve Him without fear and in holiness and righteousness; that is His will for you. That is why He let Pharaoh and his soldiers perish in the Red Sea.

God hates destiny destroyers. For this reason, when Herod wanted to kill baby Jesus, God instead saw Herod to his own pernicious end to fulfill Jesus's destiny. God hates those who use their authority to perpetrate evil, injustice, and murder. That is why God took out Jezebel. That is also why Haman, the insufferable persecutor of God's people, ended up in the gallows he had ordered for righteous Mordecai and other Jews in Persia. The weapon King Saul intended to use to kill David was eventually used to terminate his own life. Many other examples abound in the Bible; they prove that God knows how to fight for those who trust in Him with the weapons their enemies try to use against them. Herod wanted Jesus dead, but God took him out instead. Jezebel shed the blood of Naboth and took his vineyard, so God made sure Jezebel's blood was shed in the same vineyard. "Vengeance is mine," says the Lord.

However, please do not curse your enemies or wish them evil; leave that to God, who knows when the cups of your enemies are full and will fight for you. Your part is to report those destiny destroyers and unrepentant, offensive enemies to God. Ask God to avenge you. Make your case. Argue your points and present your facts to the righteous and fair Judge. I see your persecutors in trouble—the arrows they shot at you are returning to haunt them.

The Prayer Solution

- Whoever is digging malicious pits for me or any other innocent person, hear the voice of God. Repent this very moment or begin to stumble till you fall into the pit you are digging. I so decree in Jesus's name.
- Father, disappoint every spiritual weapon fashioned against me and cause my persecutors to bow to my God in Jesus's name.
- Father, keep my feet from the pits and snares of the enemy according to your Word in Jesus's name.
- Father, plead my cause and fight for me. Deliver me from forces against my soul in Jesus's name.
- Father, you are a righteous and fair judge; judge those who want me dead in Jesus's name.
- Father, by your Word, there is no rest for the wicked. Contend, O Lord, with powers spiritual or physical that contend with me in Jesus's name.
- Father, preserve my destiny from destiny destroyers in Jesus's name.

Overcoming Family Yokes

Challenges

- When there is a pattern of evil occurrences in your family. Examples are these.
    - Rejoicing is always short lived; anyone who rises soon falls.
    - A common affliction or sickness genetic or otherwise is evident.
    - A common streak of failure, poverty, or marital problems is visible.
    - A family is in decline from generation to generation.

The Word Solution

Ezekiel 18:2 says, "The fathers have eaten sour grapes and the children's teeth are set on edge." The parents had done evil, and their children were paying for it. It is a tragic situation that many families are facing today—the present generation suffering for the idolatrous sins of their ancestors. You might think this does not affect you. Not so fast, friend! Do you know what happened before your mother gave birth to you? Did your mother tell you what she went through spiritually? Did she visit a witch doctor, grove, or shrine? Did she make a sacrifice to an idol or have someone do so on her behalf?

Does your father belong to an occult group? Did he take any idolatrous chieftaincy titles? Do you know the rites involved and their implications and consequences? Can you fathom the oaths, covenants, and curses? What was the source of the money your parents used to raise you? Was it blood money, stolen cash, or cursed money?

I know a man whose late father was a witch doctor. This man fathered ten children seven of who died in his lifetime all in mysterious and sudden circumstances. The surviving three are living from hand to mouth. One is still unmarried, and two who are married are without children. It requires no seer to know that this family is under a curse. It is a problem that is common in many parts of Africa and other regions of the developing world where idol worship is still rampant. The scripturally foretold consequences of idolatry are there for all to see (Deuteronomy 5:9).

It is not rocket science to assess whether your family is free of ancestral bondage and not under a yoke or curse. A careful look at your family could reveal a pattern that can tell you all you need to know. If every branch or twig in your family tree is barely existing or surviving, that could indicate an evil spiritual climate. If no one in your family rises to prominence or anyone who rises a little falls in no time, that is an indication that God's purpose for your family is under a satanic yoke and that unseen forces of evil are having a field day at your expense. If in spite of all virtue, perseverance, and hard work, no one in your family is making any real headway in life, there may be a family curse actively at work against you all. Such an evil yoke is deadly in ways that should not be ignored. Awful and devastating consequences follow most if not all the family members in marriages, child bearing, general health, finances, and other facets of life.

In 1999, a woman came to me for prayers. She had been married for years but was without a child; she was in desperate need of one. In the course of my counseling her, she disclosed that her husband's four married brothers were childless too. It turned out that their late father had been a practicing witch doctor till his death. Our prayers broke the demonic hold of ancestral covenants and curses over their lives. By the grace of God and to the glory of our Lord Jesus Christ, childbirth became a frequent testimony of God's goodness in that family soon after.

There is hope for you too even if your family background is unclean. But first, you must locate and claim from the scriptures your right to individual freedom from the sins of your forefathers. The devil has shaped them into an ageless burden to accuse and torment your entire family. Someone in that household should stand up and read the devil the riot act of deliverance. "Thus says the Lord, the soul that sinneth, it shall die. The son shall not bear the iniquity of the Father" (Ezekiel 18:20). Thank God for this amazing revelation. You are not supposed to die for the iniquity of your parents and forebears.

This is God's Word, and its purpose must be fulfilled in the lives of those who receive it with faith and gladness of heart. Receive it now. Confess it, believe it, pray it, and stand on it. Keep praying until the yoke on your family is destroyed and you are set free. Now indeed is a door of escape open for you and yours.

The Prayer Solution

- Father, deliver me from every family yoke in Jesus's name.
- Every family curse in my life be broken in Jesus's name.
- Every evil covenant working in my family be annulled in Jesus's name.
- Every evil yoke holding my family members be broken in Jesus's name.
- Every satanic embargo placed on my family be terminated now in Jesus's name.
- Every pattern of evil in my family from today on be canceled in Jesus's name.

Power of Covenants

Challenges

- When you want guaranteed and timely answers to your prayers.
- When you want to experience the faithfulness of God in an intimate way.
- When you desire freedom from the effects of evil agreements.
- When your family's entire spiritual background requires cleansing.

The Word Solution

Written or unwritten, covenants are legal contracts with agreed-upon, binding, and enforceable terms and conditions. God is the originator of covenants; He related through them with the patriarchs of old starting with Abraham (Genesis 15:18). He sealed a covenant of nationhood in the Old Testament with the children of Jacob, whom he renamed Israel. That covenant He renewed much later as the New Testament ushered in the present time of grace for all humankind; the law and the prophets had been fulfilled by the shed blood, death, and glorious resurrection of our Lord, Jesus Christ (Hebrews 13:20).

Satan knows the power of covenants; he craftily deploys them in his dealings with his captives, agents, and associates. He seduces and commits many a naïve or unsuspecting soul to his destructive agenda and evil programs. One of his most ingenious stratagems is the use of blood covenants. Satan knows that the life of a person is in his blood (Leviticus 17:11), which by the way is the reason God says we should not eat anything with blood on it. Anyone who enters a blood covenant with or without a clear understanding of what he is doing is committing to pay with his own life for any breach of that covenant.

I recall the story of two young people who fell in love at university and entered a blood covenant; they cut themselves with a razor and licked each other's blood as they exchanged vows to marry after they graduated. They did marry as sworn, but after ten years without a child, they divorced. The man remarried, but he and his ex died within weeks of each other. Evil covenants are terrible in their exactions.

Consider on the other hand the import of a godly covenant. A good example is the one Jonathan and young David entered to protect each other from evil (1 Samuel 18:3). That saved David's life and prepared his path to the throne. Recall also the story of Hannah; she covenanted to give up her male child to the temple service of God if God would give her one to take away her reproach of barrenness. That was how Samuel became a prophet right from birth. Recall too that the covenant of God with humankind sealed by the blood of the Lamb of God has saved your soul.

In a church I was pastoring in 2000, a young woman gave a moving testimony of the covenant she had made with God in her teen years. Every Sunday, she sowed a special seed in faith that God would give her a good husband at a specified age and that she would relocate abroad with him and raise a family. At the covenanted age, she was married. She was pregnant when her husband secured a visa to a country they had always dreamed of raising their children in. Nothing is too small for you to covenant for. God indeed honors covenants (Psalm 89:34).

You must ask certain questions to locate your spiritual address with certainty. Did you in any way enter a covenant with the devil or his agents? Were you covenanted to any idol as an infant or at any stage whatsoever? Are your parents relating to any shrine in any manner? Did anyone at any time get involved in any rites on your behalf whether directly or by proxy? Is a pattern of evil discernible in your family tree suggestive of an unbroken evil covenant in your ancestral line? Such a trail may be the source of your current travails. You will need to break its power by entering a superior covenant—one sealed by Jesus's blood. If you desire something desperately, learn from Hannah—enter a covenant with God.

The Prayer Solution

- Every evil covenant inherited from my parents be broken now in Jesus's name.
- By the blood of Jesus, I renounce and revoke any pledge anyone has ever made on my behalf to any idol. In the name of Jesus, I

am free from any evil dedication made by my parents or anyone else concerning my soul, spirit, or body.

- Every covenant I entered into knowingly or unknowingly with the devil or any of his agents I renounce and break in Jesus's name.
- Father, lead me to tap into the power of genuine covenant with you in Jesus's name.
- Father, because of the covenant in the blood of Jesus, cause goodness and mercy to follow me everywhere I go in Jesus's name.
- Father, give me the grace to fulfill my obligations in every covenant I make with you in Jesus's name.
- Father, I am your covenant child; release covenant blessings to me every day in Jesus's name.

Holy Spirit Fire

Challenges

- When you need divine direction.
- When you want forces of evil put on the run.
- When you want spiritual darkness to disappear.
- When you want your spiritual environment rendered uncomfortable for demonic forces.
- When you want accelerated divine intervention against the works of the enemy.

The Word Solution

Fire has an amazing capacity to produce light and heat that can transform every substance. Wood fires give off a red flame, gas fires give off a hotter blue flame, and flames given off by fires of wax and other combustible materials give off a yellow flame. The fire welders use gives off an intense white flame. But not even this highest grade of fire can match the fire of God in intensity, power, and luminosity. This fire goes from God wherever He wants to manifest His presence.

The pillar of fire that led the children of Israel from Egypt to the Promised Land (Exodus 13:21) powerfully signified God's supremacy over all elements and conditions. God's presence in the form of fire provided the children of Israel with warmth and light during cold, dark nights. It also scared off beasts and enemies and deprived them of darkness they needed to ambush God's children.

Those benefits were so evident and vital that whenever the moving pillar of fire stayed in one place, the trekking nation stopped its journey. The same way natural fire burns paper, enemies daring to come close to the camp of Israel were be consumed by the fire of God's protective presence.

Are you troubled by any demonic agent? Command the fire of God upon them. This fire can consume evil spirits unlike natural fires, which can burn only earthly materials. Is that not why God reserved fire as the last punishment for Satan and his demons? Even now, the evil one and his camp mates cannot withstand fire. Anytime you feel a chill suggestive of an evil atmosphere, call on the Holy Spirit for the fire of His holy presence. The instant heat that will come over you will cause the lurking demons to flee. God's supernatural fire will rout evil forces at the request of His saints.

Our Lord and Savior Jesus Christ made it clear that He gave us power over serpents and scorpions and every power of the enemy (Luke 10:19). The fire of the Holy Spirit is one of the most effectual weapons for exercising that power. But only a confident child of God walking in the grace of salvation and holiness can invoke that weapon. "Deep calleth unto deep" (Psalm 42:7).

The Prayer Solution

- Holy Spirit fire, shine on me in Jesus's name.
- Fire of the Holy Spirit, confound my attackers in Jesus's name.
- Father, envelop me with the fire of the Holy Spirit in Jesus's name.
- Jesus, you are the cornerstone of my life; may your presence be a permanent pillar of fire in my family that all eyes may see your glory in us.

- Every serpent and scorpion troubling me or mine be consumed by the fire of God in Jesus's name.
- Father, protect my family with the fire of your presence today and always in Jesus's name.

Chapter 2

Success Capsules

Power of Blessings

Challenges

- When all your hard work amounts to so little.
- When you seem to be caught in a repeated cycle of failure.
- When you can't excel as others can in spite of much more effort.

The Word Solution

To be blessed means to flourish, to succeed in a remarkable or exceptional way. It also implies being divinely favored, to increase and multiply, to be above rather than below.

God's blessing confers rights to celebration, not rites of grief and mourning. The enemies of those who are blessed cannot defeat them no matter how hard they try. Those who are blessed receive divine success and excel in whatever they do.

Success does not come by hard work alone; it takes God's blessing too. His blessing is like the rain necessary for farmers to reap a bountiful harvest. When God blesses your hard work, your success is assured.

God will bless the work of your hands (Deuteronomy 28:12). The generations following those who are blessed will likewise increase and prosper. God's blessing of Isaac reflected that pattern. His son, Jacob, became highly favored as God commanded his prosperity and declared that those who cursed him would be cursed and those who blessed him would be blessed (Genesis 27:28–29). Those who are blessed are like ambassadors in foreign countries who have diplomatic immunity and privileges.

When I joined a bank some years ago as a deputy general manager, my appointment was expected to be confirmed after six months as was that of a colleague who started working at the same time. Exactly one year after, he was promoted to the general manager position but I became the executive director, a double promotion.

Friend, God can help you jump a queue without breaking the law; that is the power of His blessing. Jacob blessed Ephraim and Manasseh, the two sons of Joseph, his favored son. The two grandchildren became his adopted sons (Genesis 48:5) and thereby became patriarchs of Israel who inheriting their grandfather's eternal blessings.

There is nothing a blessed man cannot achieve, so stop struggling for success without first seeking God's blessings; they make up for what your effort alone cannot achieve. I pray that God will bless you and the work of your hands. Cry out now for God's blessing; ask Him to bless you. Esau wept when he missed the blessing of his father, Isaac. Jacob cried out to the angel of the Lord and refused to let go of Him unless He blessed him. Do not sleep tonight until you have cried out to God for His blessing.

The Prayer Solution

- Father, I need your blessings in every area of my life.
- Father, bless the work of my hands in Jesus's name.
- Father, make me a blessing to my generation in Jesus's name.
- Every curse over me, Father, break in Jesus's name.
- Father, make whoever sets out to curse me end up blessing me in Jesus's name.
- Father, command your manifold blessings on my family in Jesus's name.
- Father, as you bless me, reverse every evil in my life in Jesus's name.

Sustaining Success

Challenges

- When your career path is marred by rise and fall.
- When you lose your source of livelihood after some initial progress.
- When loss of job, wealth, or business appears imminent or inevitable.

The Word Solution

History is replete with the lives of highly successful leaders who died as failures. Today, in every city of the world, the streets are full of wretched men who were once very rich. Is it possible for a successful man to remain successful until the end of his life? Of course the answer is yes. The secret of enduring success lies in a careful study of those who maintained their success to the end. It also lies in the study of those who failed halfway to find out and avoid their mistakes.

Nebuchadnezzar was an example of pathetic failure and falling at the very peak of success. He was a world-acclaimed king who became so proud that he provoked God's anger. A glory-seeking monarch, he was turned into a wretched animal at the height of his glory; for seven years, he walked on all fours and ate grass (Daniel 5:33). Contrast this fallen royal with David, the king of Israel. The latter's success lasted to his very end and even passed on in greater measure to his son and chosen successor, Solomon. This is not to suggest that David was perfect; he made human and grievous mistakes, but he was quick to repent, confess his sins to God, and seek His forgiveness (Psalm 51:1–19). David's greatest virtue was his humility before his God. He never forgot his humble beginnings and never failed to honor God as his source and mainstay. Even as king, he danced generously for God (2 Samuel 6:14). God endorsed him and called him a man after His own heart. It is no wonder that Jesus was from the root of David.

Any river that disconnects from its source will dry up. Every wise man who wishes to be successful must remain connected to his source of success. Pride disconnects us from the source of all life—God—who resists proud people (James 4:6). It is left to us to stay connected to the source of life, to be a branch connected to God's vine (John 15:5).

Friend, never forget where you started from. Never disconnect from your source of life and success. Do not repeat or extend the bad pages of history. Look around and see how the proud and mighty are falling daily. Do not become an object of mockery. Let your success be anchored in God and be sustainable. Leave a godly inheritance for your children and their children.

I pray that your success will be recorded in good books. I pray that you will be celebrated even after you are gone to heaven. I am confident that you will choose wisely and proceed today to do the needful in order to sustain your success till the end.

The Prayer Solution

- Father, restrain me from whatever trait or attitude in me that could truncate my success in Jesus's name.
- Father, do not let me fall into the enemy's traps I pray in Jesus's name.
- Father, give me the grace of humility I need to achieve my destiny in Jesus's name.
- I reject the spirit of pride at the edge of ultimate success in Jesus's name.
- Father, sustain my success to the end in Jesus's name.
- Father, never let me fall into pride and arrogance. Keep me humble and levelheaded no matter how high you promote me in life in Jesus's name.
- Father, never let me be disconnected from you in Jesus's name.

Power to Make a Difference

Challenges

- When you want to be favored in a stiff competition.
- When you want to be highly sought after.

- When you want to make history.
- When you want to be a player rather than a spectator in the stadium of life.
- When you want to be enrolled in life's hall of fame.
- When you are tired of being average.
- When you really want to excel.
- When you desire to be celebrated.
- When you want to touch lives.

The Word Solution

Many people wonder why they fail to excel in their endeavors; they are amazed that they remain average. Some Christians even think they were destined to be small people. Some believe greatness is determined up-front by God for those He predestined for greatness.

The truth is that God is a fair judge. He is not a respecter of persons. Anyone who does His will is acceptable to Him. If someone's background predetermines his future irreversibly, then Jabez would not have become successful (1 Chronicles 4:9–10). Our destinies keep changing depending on our level of knowledge of the Word of God and our obedience to God. God can reverse Himself on our destinies; He did that to the family of Eli (1 Samuel 2:27–35).

What you will be in life depends on the choices you make today. God has kept evil and good before you; He advises you to choose good so you will live (Deuteronomy 30:15–16).

What do you see? What is the most dominant thought in your heart? What do you envision yourself achieving? Do you see what others do not? If you choose to be different, you will make a difference. Your capacity to think and act differently will make you think and act differently and produce results different from those that others produce, and you will stand out. Do you want to hide in the crowd or be on center stage?

A soccer stadium can contain a hundred thousand people, but only twenty-two can play the game. Do you want to be a player receiving applause or a spectator whom no one knows is there? If you want to make a difference, you must dare to think and act differently. Work hard at your vision. You will become different from the norm.

Jesus acted differently. He died for others. He did unusual things. He was different. He made a difference.

I see you making a difference.

The Prayer Solution

- Father, teach me to know you and love you in Jesus's name.
- Father, help me walk in obedience every day of my life in Jesus's name.
- Father, help me make a difference in my generation in Jesus's name.
- Father, cause me to excel everywhere I go in Jesus's name.
- I refuse to be a spectator in the stadium of life; I choose to be a player in Jesus's name.
- Father, let me stand out in the crowd in Jesus's name.
- Father, make me first among equals by wisdom of honest service to others in Jesus's name.

Great Grace

Challenges

- When you need divine help in career or business.
- When against all odds you aim to achieve success.
- When all hopes are lost but you still trust God to see you through.

The Word Solution

In Acts 4:33, we learn that the apostles testified of Jesus with great power and that His great grace was upon them.

There is an evident relationship between the manifestation of the power of God and the working of His grace in His children. The greater the grace of God on you, the higher the manifestation of the power of God will be through you. The gifts of the Holy Spirit are bestowed by divine grace (Ephesians 4:7).

The Bible showcases the infant Jesus waxing strong in the spirit and grace of God on Him as He grew into adolescence (Luke 2:40). Paul said that he was who he was by the grace of God (1 Corinthians 15:10). The scriptures command us to be strong in grace (2 Timothy 2:1) and recommend that we grow in grace (2 Peter 3:18).

The truth is that to be filled with power, we need to first be clean. But human righteousness is like a filthy rag, so we are justified only by grace (Romans 3:24), a virtue that we can access only through faith (Romans 5:2).

Friend, do you want to excel? Do you want to manifest God's glory and power in your daily life? You need God's grace—that is what it takes to do great things. The Lord is speaking great grace this moment, and it is available for you. Tap into it by faith. Yearn for it, pray for it, desire it. I see you walking in great grace from now on, grace that will release divine favor and enable you to enjoy the infinite blessings of open heavens.

The Prayer Solution

- Father, never let your grace run out on me in Jesus's name.
- Father, give me the grace to witness for you daily in Jesus's name.
- Father, let me experience great grace in witnessing for Christ everywhere I go in Jesus's name.
- Father, let me grow in grace every day of my life in Jesus's name.
- Father, help me be strong in grace in Jesus's name.
- Father, let your grace make way for my needs and desires in Jesus's name.

Performance of Prophecies

Challenges

- When there is delayed manifestation of prophesied and awaited favors.
- When you long to see fulfillment of prophecy.

The Word Solution

There is often a time lag between a prophecy and its manifestation. If God says He will do anything, He will do it but only at His appointed time, which might not be immediately. He might delay a prophecy's fulfillment for many reasons; He might be teaching the believer the virtues of total trust and enduring patience, or perhaps the circumstances to preface the event are evolving.

One of the most challenging tasks for most human beings is to wait, but for those who walk with God, waiting is imperative; He promises to reward with strength and renewal those who wait on Him (Isaiah 40:31). The good news about God's promise is that it will certainly come to pass. Waiting for its performance is therefore an act and test of faith. The challenge is that in most cases, we may not know the appointed time.

What has God promised you that is yet to manifest? Whether it comes by dream, vision, or prophetic utterance, God's promise cannot fail no matter how long it tarries. The Bible makes it clear that concerning the chosen vessel for the virgin birth that would redeem all humankind, "Blessed is she that believed: for there shall be a performance of those things which were told her from the Lord" (Luke 1:45).

God is not a man who can lie. He brings to pass whatever He promises. Paul told the Roman believers that God would perform whatever He promised (Romans 4:21). God said through Jeremiah that He would perform what He promised (Jeremiah 33:14).

Do you desire a speedy manifestation of the promises God has made to you? Remind God about them because every prophecy is a prayer point. In the words of Paul to Timothy, "War a good warfare" with the prophecies that were spoken over your life (1 Timothy 1:18).

Ask for more grace to wait for the appointed time. Do not just fold your hands; according to the Bible, the vision is for an appointed time, so we must write it down and run with it (Habakkuk 2:2–3).

I see an accelerated manifestation of divine promises in your favor.

The Prayer Solution

- Every delay in the fulfillment of my God-given prophecies be terminated now in Jesus's name.
- All forces against the manifestation of God's prophecies in my life, Father, confound in Jesus's name.
- Concerning the timely manifestation of your promises to me, Father, reveal and enable me to perform my own part of any obligation in Jesus's name.
- Father, grant me the blessed patience to wait for your divine timing concerning the manifestation of prophecies in Jesus's name.
- Father, teach me every lesson I need to learn for your prophecies to be fulfilled in my life in Jesus's name.
- Father, by your grace, shorten the waiting time for the manifestation of my miracles in Jesus's name.

Overcoming by the Spirit

Challenges

- When flesh rules your thoughts and habits.
- When your fleshly lusts seem insurmountable.
- When your earnest desire is to live a victorious life of holiness.

The Word Solution

You are a human being. You live in the flesh, but you are also soul and spirit. Your flesh desires food, water, honor, position, wealth, and so on. Unfortunately, the desires of your flesh are often contrary to what God's Spirit yearns for in you. God, the Holy Spirit, lives in your spirit when you are born again. And just as your body needs food, your spirit should be fed with the Word of God, prayer, communion, and fellowship with the brethren for you to grow as God's child.

The desires of the flesh and those of the Spirit run contrary to one another according to the Bible; the flesh is at war with the Spirit. Galatians

5:17 reads, "The flesh lusted against the Spirit and the Spirit against the flesh: and these are contrary the one to the other: so that ye cannot do the things you would."

Without the indwelling Spirit, you cannot please God or do what He wants you to do (Philippians 2:13). Because God is a Spirit, you cannot worship Him except in spirit and truth (John 4:24). The Bible exhorts us to control the flesh by mortifying the deeds thereof (Romans 8:13), and Paul showed us a worthy personal example (1 Corinthians 9:27). Since God is Spirit, there is no godly success for anyone outside a life lived in the Spirit.

Stop struggling for success in the flesh. Ask instead for a baptism of the Holy Spirit. Jesus instructed His apostles to tarry in Jerusalem until they received the Holy Spirit (Luke 24:49).

Live in the Spirit. Feed your spirit with prayer, Bible study, praises, and worship of God. Give time to regular fellowship with the brethren, and live in complete and unquestioning obedience to the Word of God. Fast occasionally (deny your body food and drink) in cognitive acceptance that we do not live by bread alone. That is how to crucify your flesh, deliver yourself from fleshly lusts, and gain self-discipline, which never offend God. You will thereby war, work, and live in the Spirit and abound in testimonies.

The Prayer Solution

- Father, help me desire regular nourishment for my spirit in Jesus's name.
- Father, help me to overcome the sinful lusts of the flesh in Jesus's name.
- Father, may I be led and guided by your Spirit and never by the flesh in Jesus's name.
- Holy Spirit, help me crucify my flesh daily in Jesus's name.
- Father, help me walk in obedience to your Spirit always in Jesus's name.
- Father, help me keep my body under subjection to your Spirit in me in Jesus's name.
- Whatever it takes to live in the Spirit, Father, give me in Jesus's name.

Courage for Exploits

Challenges

- When you face strong opposition and need divine grace to surmount it.
- When you are confronted by a mountain of problems blocking your aspirations.
- When you are troubled by an overwhelming sense of fear or inadequacy in your quest for success.

The Word Solution

Fainthearted people cannot reach the top. Great men and women are always courageous, and no one who is afraid of confronting opposition can make history. Great people look forward to confronting and overcoming obstacles and challenges on their way up because they know that promotion follows when they overcome their challenges.

A multimillionaire friend told me that every new problem he encounters in his business gives him a thrill. This is because most often, every seemingly difficult thing is the last impediment to amazing success. He also believes firmly that there is no obstacle that is insurmountable.

The biblical David was a courageous boy. While his countrymen cowered in fear before Goliath, David ran to engage him in mortal combat (1 Samuel 17:48). Shadrach, Meshach, and Abednego were three outstanding youths of Judah who like Daniel distinguished themselves in their Babylonian captivity. They were bold and minced no words in rejection of the idolatrous King Nebuchadnezzar's overtures (Daniel 3:16). God rewarded their exemplary courage with unparalleled exploits that became a testimony to all generations.

Moses was raised as an Egyptian prince in Pharaoh's palace. But after years of self-exile born of fear for his life, he returned with an outrageously courageous demand on Pharaoh (Exodus 5:1); his bold and persistent petition, "Let my people go," was the key that unlocked historic events and exploits that would earn him an immortal place in the history of God's people. In later years, God instruct Joshua, his successor, to be courageous if he wanted to succeed as Moses had (Joshua 1:6).

Do not be afraid of your challenges. Look forward to your battles. Be courageous and holy. God will back you up, and you will be promoted all the way to the top.

The Prayer Solution

- Father, take away doubt and fear from my life in Jesus's name.
- Father, make me as strong and as bold as a lion in Jesus's name.
- Father, strengthen me and equip me with courage to confront every obstacle in my way in Jesus's name.
- I declare today that I receive the spirit of courage and confidence in Jesus's name.
- Father, help me realize who I am in you in Jesus's name.
- I overcome whatever fear in me today in Jesus's name.
- Because I am more than a conqueror through Christ, I fear no opposition any more in Jesus's name.

Power of Divine Counsel

Challenges

- When you are tired of deceptive or unhelpful advice from others.
- When you desire superior counsel about the issues of life.
- When you cannot tell which counsel will guarantee good results.

The Word Solution

No one succeeds in life without good advisers because no one knows it all, not even the so-called professionals and experts who at best specialize only in their narrow disciplines. We all need others to better ourselves. The best doctor might need a smart lawyer, and that lawyer might need a good financial advisor, and so on.

Our ability to achieve depends on the quality of the counsel we receive. And failure can be traced to wrong advice or the wrong adviser even if we received that from someone who did so in goodwill. It may have come from sheer incompetence, but the result is the same—a calamity even with the best of intentions.

Good advice is as critical as a good foundation for a house is. A faulty foundation threatens the whole house. So it is with our lives. Absalom, the favorite son of King David, failed in his premature bid for his father's throne. His coup was an initial success, but in the end, he died before his time because he had listened to wrong advice and ignored the wise counsel of Ahitophel (2 Samuel 17:7). His nephew, Rehoboam, paid a price for listening to the rash counsel of his fellow youths rather than the sober counsel of his elders; his nascent regime suffered an irreversible breakup of Israel into two kingdoms (1 Kings 12:8).

You need a counselor who cannot mislead you. You need a counselor who cannot be bought by your enemies. You need a counselor who is knowledgeable and from whom nothing is hidden. His name is Jesus. The Bible calls Him the wonderful counselor (Isaiah 9:6).

Never make a major decision without consulting Jesus, the wonderful counselor. If you call on Him, He will answer you and show you amazing secrets (Jeremiah 33:3). You will not make mistakes if you rely on divine counsel.

May our God answer you today.

The Prayer Solution

- Every evil counsel that I ever acted upon, Father, help me turn away from completely in Jesus's name.
- Are there evil counselors in my life? Father, expose them and separate me from them in Jesus's name.
- Father, give me the grace to discern good counsel from evil in Jesus's name.
- Father, make me a godly counselor in every situation in Jesus's name.
- Lord Jesus, you are the wonderful counselor. Make me attentive to your loving counsel so I can please you in all things in your name.

- Father, I resolve today never again to take a major decision without obtaining your counsel in Jesus's name.
- Every counsel I need to achieve my destiny, Father, cause me to receive in Jesus's name.

The Power of Friendship

Challenges

- When you are involved in wrong friendships.
- When you desire good associates and friends who will add value to your life.
- When you are tired of working alone and desire godly relationships.

The Word Solution

Achieving your destiny depends in part on who your friends and associates are. Friendship is a powerful influence for good or evil. Associates contribute profoundly to your thinking, behavior, and actions. You may not realize it, but in many ways, you are a product of your friendships. Godly friends help you with godly counsel just as ungodly friends might you with their demonic counsel. In the words of our Lord, Jesus Christ, a good tree yields good fruit; conversely, a corrupt tree bears only corrupt fruit.

Even more than the effect of spoken words is the power of character. The behavior of our closest friends influences our conduct so much that we often end up doing exactly what they do. Every human being is a copycat for good or bad.

Consider the biblical story of David. The human instrument God used to bring him to the throne of Israel was Jonathan, the heir apparent to that throne. Jonathan was the first son of Saul, the incumbent king, and he wore the royal belt he was entitled to wear as the crown prince. But he symbolically handed it over to his bosom friend David desiring David to take the throne in his place. At the risk of his own life, he provided David with highly classified information that helped save his life. Jonathan was a friend indeed; David's lament at his death said it all.

Consider also the story of King Rehoboam, who listened to counsel that tore Israel apart (2 Chronicles 10:11–14). In Proverbs 13:20 (KJV), we read, "He that walketh with wise men shall be wise: but a companion of fools shall be destroyed." Equally succinct are the blessings in Psalm 1:1–3 concerning refusing to accept ungodly counsel and to hobnob with sinners and the scornful and thus not ending up as "chaff that the wind drives away" (Psalm 1:4).

One married woman had a best friend, a single woman. She shared her every thought and trouble with her especially her frequent spats with her husband. Her confidante opined that she was stomaching too much disrespect from her husband and letting herself be taken for granted for too long. The friend told her to leave her home and let her husband miss her for a time; she said he would come begging for her to return and she could then lay down new conditions for the marriage. The gullible woman moved out, and her best friend moved in the very same night and became the husband's new wife.

Who are your best friends? Whom do you hang out with? Whom do you chat with on Whatsap? Whom do you follow on Twitter and Instagram? Who are your friends on Facebook? Whom do you exchange emails and messages with? Whom do you visit? Whom do you call frequently? Scroll down your call log and find that out. They are your friends most likely; they have a lot of influence on you consciously and unconsciously and are either diminishing your worth or adding value to you. Your friends affect your destiny for good or bad.

Friend, so much is at stake in the friendships we make, maintain, lose, or forsake. Wisdom will cause us to reject relationships that undermine our destiny in Christ. Only friendships that enhance our spirituality ought to be maintained. It boils down to choices and the grace to discern that we all must pray for.

In the spring of 2000, I was waiting for my luggage at the airport in Lagos; I had just come back from a trip to New York. I struck up a conversation with a man, and we ended up exchanging business cards. We didn't know that God had just united two hearts in a lifelong friendship that would prove such a great blessing.

He was a Christian pastor and an engineer. He had just retired from a leading oil and gas company and was about to vacate his old house for a new one. On learning that I was searching for accommodations, he promptly offered me the use of his older house. He went beyond that; he offered to arrange for me to buy a property near his new house. He and I have been friends for over nineteen years now. He is still my neighbor, friend, mentor, and pastor. Pray that God will send you godly friends like that.

Remove bad friends from your life; delete their phone numbers and email addresses and replace them with godly friends. Things will rapidly change in your favor thereafter.

The Prayer Solution

- Father, disconnect me from evil friends and associates in Jesus's name.
- Any friendship that results in a spiritual deficit, Father, separate me from in Jesus's name.
- Every evil, vice, wickedness, folly, and fraud that is deceptively packaged as friendship, Father, expose to me in Jesus's name.
- Father, give me grace to discern and avoid evil friendship in Jesus's name.
- Father, bless me with a Jonathan, a true friend and brother in one person in Jesus's name.
- Father, give me the courage to walk away from relationships that are of no benefit in Jesus's name.

Power of Vows

Challenges

- When you desire guaranteed answer to your prayers.
- When you wish to experience the faithfulness of God as a covenant keeper.
- When you have prayed and fasted yet your problems remain unsolved.

The Word Solution

A vow is an oath, an irrevocable promise to do something, a solemn and binding commitment. People make vows to one another for instance when they marry to love and live with each other until death. Government officials take vows when they are sworn into office.

By their nature, vows are never supposed to be broken by anyone who made them. A vow made to God is even more irreversible. It is a sin to break it (Deuteronomy 23:21). On the other hand, fulfilling it results in a divine guarantee that God will do His part of the covenant.

In the Bible, everyone who made a vow to God received what he or she desired. After many years of prayer at Shiloh, Hannah changed her prayer style. She made a vow to give back to God the son she was asking Him to give her (1 Samuel 1:11). God responded to that vow and gave her Samuel. When she fulfilled her vow, God gave her five more children.

Jephthah made a vow to God, and God gave him a resounding victory over the enemies of Israel (Judges 11:30). Jacob made a vow to God, and God protected him and blessed him mightily (Genesis 28:20). What do you desire from the Lord that as Hannah did you have prayed or even wept for without a result? Have you gone through weeks and months of praise and worship but God has not moved on the matter? Consider making a vow to Him. Tell God what you will do for Him if He gives you what you are asking for. Be sure to promise only what you can do. Be sure too that your vow will benefit God and His kingdom. Wisely make a vow, and you will witness a miracle.

Some years ago, I made a vow to God and asked for many things in return. By the grace of God, one of the many fruits of that vow is the anointing for this book. I have received countless other wonderful dividends for making that vow, and sorrows have turned to joy in many families including mine. If you need major help from God but your prayers have yielded no answer, it may be time to make a vow.

The Prayer Solution

- Every vow I have consciously or unguardedly made to the devil I revoke in Jesus's name.
- Blood of Jesus, nullify every curse arising from any vow or token of allegiance made wittingly or unwittingly by me or by anyone else on my behalf to any evil spirit.
- Father, teach me how to make and honor my vows in Jesus's name.
- Father, I pray in particular to fulfill my marital vow to the very end in Jesus's name.
- Father, deliver me from the vows of death in Jesus's name.

Make a vow now to God, but be careful to vow only what you can do. Ask for something in return.

Know Who You Are: Destiny's Child

Challenges

- When you wish to know why you were born.
- When you want to fulfill your destiny.
- When you want to conquer every opposition to your destiny.

The Word Solution

Every child is born to fulfill a peculiar purpose and should not be a mere spectator in the theater of life. No one is meant to be lost in the crowd or to just clap and applaud others who are making something of their lives.

Moses was a child of destiny. Some other children born at the time of his birth were killed. He survived against all odds. He still led over a million people on foot out of the land of the oppressors. God used him to do great signs including crossing the Red Sea.

Joseph, Daniel, and Joshua were all children of destiny. God told Jeremiah that he was chosen and anointed before he was born (Jeremiah

1:5). Every born-again child of God is a child of destiny meant to reign and rule.

You are part of a holy nation. You are a peculiar person. You are a royal priesthood. As will every child of destiny, you will experience opposition and challenges, but you will overcome them. God will release uncommon grace on you, and divine assistance will come your way.

Now that you know who you are, go for the best. Do not accept playing second fiddle. Do not accept inferior positions or allow yourself to be discouraged by any opposition. Be conscious of your purpose on earth, and be determined to achieve it. If you do not fulfill the purpose for which you were born, you will disappoint God as well as yourself.

I am confident that with the help of God, you will fulfill your destiny.

The Prayer Solution

- Father, every obstacle to my destiny please remove in Jesus's name.
- Every power opposing the will of God for me be dethroned in Jesus's name.
- Father, reveal to me the purpose for which I was born in Jesus's name.
- Father, may I not be a spectator in my life in Jesus's name. Father, distinguish me among my peers in Jesus's name.
- Father, give me uncommon grace to fulfill my destiny in Jesus's name.

Power of Thanksgiving

Challenges

- When you want the gates of heaven to open for you.
- When you desire uncommon miracles.
- When you need access to the throne room of God.
- When you desire the resurrection power of Christ in business, career, family, or other relationships.

The Word Solution

We find it easy to thank God when we have breakthroughs; it would seem absurd to thank God when things are not going our way. But the scriptures expressly command us to thank God "in all things" (1 Thessalonians 5:18).

Thanking God even when there is unpleasant news or outcomes is an act of worship that moves His heart. In 1999, my first son died. That night, I worshipped God with a bleeding heart. I reminded Him of His words. I was weeping yet thanking Him. That night, God spoke to me in a vision and gave me many promises. The years that followed brought fulfillment of all His promises plus another son, who is an exact replica of his departed brother.

Consider the time the Lord Jesus Christ preached many days in the wilderness to a great multitude. At the end of the long event, He was concerned that there was nowhere the people could buy something to eat. He also knew that a homeward journey would be tough for most of the people as they had not eaten for days. A small boy's lunch of two fishes and five loaves of bread was presented to Him, but how on earth was that supposed to feed the five thousand men there let alone their women and children?

What Jesus did was noteworthy. He lifted the grossly insufficient meal up to heaven and thanked God for it (Matthew 15:36). That act of thanksgiving opened the heavens. The fish and bread began to multiply. The rest is history.

Consider also the story of Lazarus, who was dead and had been in the grave for four days. Decay had already set in. In the eyes of man, that was a closed chapter, a hopeless case. But Jesus arrived. He too wept on the scene, but unlike all the other mourners, He looked up to heaven and thanked God for the remains of his friend, Lazarus. He then issued a command. The rest is history (John 11:41).

Is there an ostensibly hopeless case in your life? Is there a patent defect, a crucial lack, or a gross insufficiency troubling you? You may have prayed long over the matter, spent sleepless nights, and even sought great men and women of God to intercede for you but to no avail. Have you considered rendering thanks for that problem? That may sound ridiculous, but God uses ridiculous things to do miraculous things. God uses foolish things to confound the wise (1 Corinthians 1:27).

Thanking God for that problem will open the heavens for you (Psalm 100:4) and provoke divine compassion in your favor.

As you thank God intensely even for a problem, I see the heavens giving you attention. I see divine intervention coming your way resulting in a total turnaround of even seemingly impossible situations. Let God be magnified.

The Prayer Solution

- Father, forgive my not thanking you enough for all you have been doing for me in Jesus's name.
- Father, accept my thanks for all you have done for me in Jesus's name.
- Father, I thank you for what you are doing this moment for me in Jesus's name even as I acknowledge that there is none alive who knows or appreciates how great your favors and mercies to man are.
- Father, I thank you for all my prayers you have answered in Jesus's name. Father, I thank you also for all my prayers that are awaiting your answer in Jesus's name. Father, your word says we should give thanks in all things. I thank you, Lord, even for all the pains and griefs I have experienced in Jesus's name.
- Father, as I thank you now, may the heavens open for me.

Would you spend the next half an hour thanking God?

Power of Divine Helpers

Challenges

- When you really need assistance to succeed.
- When you feel the best you have done is not good enough.
- When you need a useful contact or connection.

The Word Solution

There is a limit to what you can achieve by yourself; success is much easier when you have helpers. Consider David. God raised Jonathan from inside the enemy camp to help him. If Jonathan had not provided David with information to aid his escape, Saul, Jonathan's father, would have killed David.

Consider how Esther became a queen in a foreign country where she was officially a captive slave like the rest of her kindred, the Jews. Even though her curriculum vitae did not qualify her for that coveted position, it pleased God to raise helpers for her. Her uncle, Mordecai, a gate man at the palace, was privy to privileged information that he wisely passed on to her. She also received help throughout the screening process from the organizers of the pageant as God caused them to favor her. She was elevated to a royal position, and God used her in that office as a divine helper to save Israel from the genocidal machinations of the wicked Haman.

Consider Joseph, a young lad who would have died in jail if God had not raised his former prison mate as a divine helper for him. God caused Pharaoh to have a dream that no one in the palace could interpret. It was in the ensuing impasse that the king's butler, Joseph's erstwhile fellow prisoner, put in a good word for Joseph that enabled him to showcase his gift before Pharaoh. Joseph the prisoner became Joseph the prime minister.

You need people to connect you to the top or help you out of trouble. It may not be the people you expect God will use, but ask God for helpers. He has already prepared them, and He will surely connect you to them.

Years ago, I had some training in some banks in New York and Philadelphia. It was an all-expenses paid program underwritten by the US government. I never knew that such a scholarship existed. God simply raised a helper who secured the application form and sent it to me. I applied and was awarded the scholarship. The training changed my resume.

I pray that God will send you divine helpers.

The Prayer Solution

- Father, as you did for the Jews in Babylon, raise an Esther for me in Jesus's name.
- Father, command men and women to help me everywhere I go in Jesus's name.
- Any power or spirit contending against my divinely appointed helpers I bind and cast out in Jesus's name.
- Father, send divine helpers my way daily in Jesus's name.
- Father, connect me to every helper you have appointed for me in Jesus's name.
- Whatever my duties to my divine helpers are, Father, reveal and direct me to do them in Jesus's name.
- Father, even from within my enemies' camp, raise divine helpers for me in Jesus's name.

Power of Divine Wisdom

Challenges

- When you are weary to the bone or feeling extremely frustrated.
- When you don't know what to say or do to extricate yourself from a difficult circumstance.
- When you can't figure out a solution for a difficult problem.
- When human knowledge and intellectual power are failing you.

The Word Solution

The opposite of foolishness is wisdom. Foolish actions produce unprofitable results. Every problem in life can be solved with wisdom. Wisdom equips you with the right word or action to get you out of any fix. Very often, wisdom is the difference between success and failure. That is why the Bible says that wisdom is the principal thing (Proverbs 4:7).

Wisdom is a big help when you come under the enemy's attack (Ecclesiastes 7:12). Your enemy's strength becomes useless when you confront him with wisdom. Wisdom is better than strength (Ecclesiastes 9:16).

Wisdom can overcome poverty; it can guide you to wealth. The Bible says wisdom is better than gold (Proverbs 16:6). Wisdom is so important that it was recorded in the Bible that Jesus grew in it (Luke 2:52).

What are the challenges facing your marriage today? Divine wisdom will solve those quarrels between you and your spouse. You need God's grace to handle your issues be they business, marital, social, or other. Grace enables you to relate better with all the people in your life. Show me someone at loggerheads with others and I will show you a person who lacks divine wisdom.

Your business may stagnate if you lack the wisdom to run it well. You may not be able to move to the next level unless you find wisdom. Ask God for wisdom today. God promised to give wisdom to those who asked for it (James 1:5). The Lord gives wisdom out of His mouth (Psalm 136:5).

Wisdom comes along with the unbelievable power in listening. Wise people talk less and listen more. I have since learned that I need not talk in every meeting. The Holy Spirit will tell you when to listen and when to talk.

The fear of God is the beginning of wisdom (Psalm 111:10). You are so close to the solution you have been seeking for so long. Wisdom is the key that unlocks unimaginable treasures. It comes by living a life that recognizes and reverences your Maker.

Ask God for wisdom today. He will answer, and what you seek will be yours.

The Prayer Solution

- I refuse to be a fool, so help me, God, in Jesus's name.
- Father, give me the Spirit of wisdom in Jesus's name.
- Father, increase me in wisdom daily in Jesus's name.
- Father, I desire divine wisdom; please give it to me today in Jesus's name.
- Father, help me live a holy life and fear no one but you in Jesus's name.
- Father, connect me with wise counsel and let me walk in it always in Jesus's name.

Power in the Word

Challenges

- When you desperately need solutions to lingering problems.
- When you desire guaranteed answers to your prayers.
- When you want to praise God and experience His presence.
- When all human helpers have failed you.

The Word Solution

The Word of God has immense power. The Word is God (John 1:1). It has been there from the beginning of time and will always be. Everything God did in creation was by His Word. Thousands of years into the evolving history of the human race, God's Word took on the form of man (John 1:12) and dwelled on earth. Healings and deliverances were wrought and are still being performed by the Word of God (Psalm 107:20). Everything in this world will pass away, but the Word of God can never fail. God's Word is infallible; He who promised is faithful to deliver on whatever He has promised.

Every problem on earth has a solution in the Word of God. Any unresolved problem is due only to one's inability to locate the relevant key in the Word of God. This book is all about solutions using the Word of God.

Search the scriptures for them; in them you will have life. Every word of God is backed by a divine oath; it is a covenant between humanity and God that He will never break (Psalm 89:34).

How have you tried to solve your problems? Your Creator prepared the solutions to your problems before you were even born. It is all there in the Word of God, the Bible. That book is a complete solution package waiting for you to draw from and live by.

Handling the Word of God requires wisdom and understanding, which are God's gifts to us. The scriptures make it perfectly clear that God's Word profits those who mix it with faith. Failure to apply it with faith does you no good. Faith results in obedience, another key attribute of a worshipful heart that God rewards with His manifold blessings.

Friend, your prayers are more potent if you base them on the Word of God. Have you tried locating your prayer points from the written Word of God? I do not know any prayer I have prayed from the Word of God that did not produce results.

In a recent dream, a demonic principality was chasing me around with evident intent to kill me. I woke up in fright, but God spoke an instant word to my heart and showed me by a Bible verse (Numbers 23:8) that nobody can curse or defy me because He had neither cursed nor defied me. I was pleasantly surprised that God told me not to even bother to pray about the matter, a remarkable instance of victory gained by simply believing God's Word.

About ten years ago, my cousin's wife complained of incessant nightmares that caused her lots of sleepless nights and hours spent in anguished prayer against perceived and unknown enemies. That persisted for months and left her frustrated and wondering why her prayers were not working. I was led to share with her Isaiah 4:5–6, in which God promised that His glory would be our defense. Her nightly prayer was for God's glory be released to serve as her defense as she slept. She testified that the nightmares came to an immediate end.

How do you praise God? What type of worship do you offer Him? Have you ever tried to praise Him using His Word? Try that, and His presence will invade your place of prayer.

Complaining about your problems will not solve them. Pick up your Bible as if it were an instruction manual and follow the manufacturer's instructions. Praise God with His Word. The solution to your problem is fully there.

The Prayer Solution

- Father, open my eyes to the power of solutions in your Word in Jesus's name.
- Father, enable me to pray according to your Word in Jesus's name.
- Father, move my heart to appreciate the depths of your Word so I may reverence you with praise and worship songs out of your Word in Jesus's name.
- Father, strengthen my faith in your Word in Jesus's name.

- Father, may your Word become a wonder-working force in my life in Jesus's name.
- Father, I repent of past murmurings and grumblings and ask for your forgiveness in Jesus's name.

Identify and write down promises in the Bible relating to your present needs, and pray them into manifestation calling on the name of Jesus.

Divine Favor

Challenges

- When you want God's face to shine on you.
- When you desire your good works to be remembered and rewarded.
- When you want the face of God to shine on your family.
- When you want God to take away your reproach.
- When you desperately want your prayers to be answered.

The Word Solution

It is impossible for God to forget anybody. A woman can forget her child, but God will never forget His (Isaiah 49:15). God has the capacity to remember everything about everybody all the time and forever. Yet the Bible often talks about God remembering someone. That is a manner of speaking that describes a major change or turnaround.

Whenever the Bible refers to God remembering someone, it means that God has decided to favor him in a significant way by paying special attention to that person. When God visits you with a special favor, He is said to have remembered you. Everyone has a day of divine encounter, a day of divine favor. The truth is that God listens to every prayer. "He who planted the ear, will he not hear?" (Psalm 94:9).

God is sovereign; He chooses when to respond to prayers. You can however hasten His choice of a day by making importunate prayer for His favor. God could be moved to change His mind on a matter by desperate prayer as shown in many ways in the Bible. God remembered Abraham as His friend as He moved to destroy Sodom and Gomorrah. For his sake, God spared his nephew, Lot, and his family (Genesis 19:29). Another good example is Rachael. God remembered her (Genesis 30:22), and she conceived and gave birth to Joseph. The point to note is that the moment God remembers anyone, his or her afflictions end.

Years ago, I needed a loan to purchase a property. God caused my employers to lift the embargo on loans to staff members, and I received one. Not long after I got the loan and secured the property, the embargo was reinstated.

When in need, cry out to God to favor you. He will surely look on you and visit as He promised He would.

The Prayer Solution

- Father, everywhere I go, let your favor go with in Jesus's name.
- Father, may every document I present elicit your favor in Jesus's name.
- Father, grant me the favor of worthy men and women in Jesus's name.
- Father, let your favor make a way for me in Jesus's name.
- Father, never let me lose your favor in Jesus's name.
- Father, help me to grow in favor as I grow in age in Jesus's name.
- Father, remember me for good, and may this be your set time to favor me in Jesus's name.

Chapter 3

Promotion Capsules

Uncommon Promotions

Challenges

- When you desire to be promoted in an extraordinary manner.
- When you have no human helper to help you progress your career.

The Word Solution

It is not an unusual career progression for a general manager to be elevated to executive director or a deputy manager to be promoted to manager. And there is nothing extraordinary if someone with high-level connections gains a public office appointment or a young professional with a master's degree from an Ivy League school lands a plum job in a major company.

However, consider an orphan girl whose situation is no better than that of a penniless slave. She is living with her uncle in a refugee camp, one of millions of foreigners fleeing the ravages of war in her homeland. A menial job as a housemaid anywhere would have been a huge cause for special thanksgiving, and a day in the king's palace as a cleaner would have been unthinkable. But she did become the first lady, and she reigned as queen with her husband, the king. That is the amazing story of Esther, to whom a whole book of the Bible is dedicated. It is a story of amazing grace that illustrates what can happen to anyone when God's hand is upon him or her.

The story of my life is in some ways similar to Esther's. My parents were poor and illiterate. I got through university with huge assistance from close relatives, but I had no connections who were in positions of power or privilege. Nonetheless, against all odds, at the young age of forty, I was already sitting on the board of a rising bank. Everything I got was by divine recommendation.

When I was interviewed for the job, the directors asked me who had recommended me to the bank. I told them that God had, that He had shown me a vision in a dream that I shared with them. They laughed it off but hired me. They appointed me as a director of that bank in under a year.

If your resume is as appalling as Esther's was, all you need is God's grace, the sort that enabled her to find favor with the palace officials (Esther 2:15) for you to make progress. Her move from the back bench of obscurity to the front seat and spotlight of prominence did not come by chance. She was committed to prayer and fasting. Her immortal words have inspired generations of martyrs and missionaries: "If I perish I perish" (Esther 4:16). Her life story provides a classical illustration that promotion does not come from the east or west or south but from God (Psalm 75:6).

Divine favor opens the door for promotion. I see God rewriting your resume as He did Esther's resulting in an unexpected and uncommon promotion. You will soon be celebrated, amen.

The Prayer Solution

- Father, rewrite and upscale my resume in Jesus's name.
- Anything not pleasant in my background, Father, reverse in Jesus's name.
- Father, wherever I find myself, clothe me with favor in Jesus's name.
- Father, I've heard of amazing grace. May I experience it in Jesus's name.

- Father, grant me uncommon promotion spiritually and materially in Jesus's name.
- Father, grant me a massive leap forward and cause me to be celebrated in Jesus's name.

Power of Dreams and Visions

Challenges

- When you dream but do not understand it.
- When you do not dream for months or years.
- When you dream but forget them.
- When you dream but take it lightly or ignore the signs and warnings.

The Word Solution

Christians often dream and see visions. Dreams are spiritual mysteries. Generally, they require spiritual interpretation as most dreams are not supposed to be taken literally. The spiritually immature or ignorant tend to dismiss dreams as meaningless wandering of the subconscious. But believers well grounded on scriptural truths appreciate the special spiritual significance of dreams as channels of divine revelation. When Joseph dreamed, nobody in his family dismissed it (Genesis 37:11); his dreams came to pass. When Pharaoh had a troubling dream and needed a credible interpreter, he found Joseph (Genesis 41:15). As well, Daniel interpreted the dream of King Nebuchadnezzar (Daniel 2:24).

Some people tend to dismiss dreams and especially nightmares, but every dream has a spiritual significance part of which may manifest in the physical and at times with severe consequences. Not all dreams come from God. Some are from the satanic arsenal for the deception and destruction of unguarded souls.

God said that in the last days, He would talk to His people through dreams and visions (Joel 2:28). The last days are here.

In 2002, I was working at a medium-sized bank. One day in traffic, I spotted a lovely car that I immediately fell in love with. I wished I could afford to buy a beauty like that. That night, I had a dream in which I saw a reference to Psalm 84:11 on TV. When I woke up, I remembered the dream and checked out that verse: "The Lord God is a sun and shield: the Lord will give grace and glory: no good thing will he withhold from them that walk uprightly." Less than two weeks after that, the board of directors of my bank chose that car as the official car for each of us seven who made up the senior management cadre. The one allocated to me was black, the same as the one I had seen.

What are your dreams like? Do you ignore them? Do you lack knowledge of the principles for interpreting them? Do you forget your dreams when you wake up? Do you dream at all? Whatever category you fall in, you need the infilling and baptism of the Holy Spirit as promised by our Savior (Luke 3:16). Only with the Holy Spirit poured out on you can you dream God-given dreams and see God-directed visions (Joel 2:28). Rise and take control of your life.

Nothing happens in the physical without its prior run in the spiritual realm. Dreams and visions are channels to the spiritual. They provide true believers with working platforms to shape or reshape their destiny.

You too can take control of the spiritual, reject evil dreams through prayer, and pray good visions into manifestation.

The Prayer Solution

- Father, baptize me afresh with the Holy Spirit in Jesus's name.
- Every evil dream concerning my family I cancel in Jesus's name.
- Father, cause every good dream about my future to manifest in Jesus's name.
- Father, give me the gift of interpretation of dreams in Jesus's name.
- Father, help me understand when you speak to me through dreams in Jesus's name.
- With every dream requiring action on my part, Father, direct my every step in doing all I need to do in Jesus's name.
- Father, help me overcome whatever sin of commission or omission that opens the door to satanic dreams in my life in Jesus's name.

Moving to the Next Level

Challenges

- When you desire extraordinary promotion.
- When you want to move to the next level.
- When there are obstacles and limitations blocking your promotion.
- When you want special promotion despite your admitted limitations.
- When you desire to be promoted against all odds or limitations.

The Word Solution

God desires His children to progress and succeed, increase and multiply. In the words of the psalmist, King David, "The Lord shall increase you more and more, you and your children" (Psalm 115:14). God is eager to see you at a higher level in terms of health and finances. Your stagnation or failure does not glorify God; He loves seeing you promoted.

If you desire divine promotion, you must first appreciate that God's season for promotion is here and now. If you understand that, look to Him, not any person. Put no trust in man for man will fail you. Man is limited in goodwill, goodness, scope, and ability to help himself and others. That is why Psalm 75:6 declares that promotion comes only from God. He is the power than can lift one up and bring another down. He is the one who lifts up a beggar from the dunghill and seats him with princes (1 Samuel 2:8).

To gain your rightful place in His thoughts, you must live a holy life. He blesses those who fear Him (Psalm 115:13).

There is still room at the top for you. I see God moving you to the next level. Welcome to divine promotion!

The Prayer Solution

- Father, terminate every form of stagnancy in my life today in Jesus's name.
- Every embargo over my promotion, Father, cause to be lifted in Jesus's name.
- Father, promote me in every aspect of life in Jesus's name.
- Unseat any usurper of my God-given position, Father, in Jesus's name.
- Father, increase me on all sides in Jesus's name.
- Father, reveal to me whatever I am required to do and equip me to do it creditably in Jesus's name.
- Father, may visible divine promotion advertise your glory in my life in Jesus's name.

Anointed to Reign

Challenges

- When you are tired of feeling small.
- When you are feeling inferior.
- When you ought to be in charge but feel you can't.
- When you are tired of being under.

The Word Solution

Many a believer has been bombarded with wrong teachings. Some think that playing second fiddle or settling for an inferior position is a mark of humility, but it is not. Knuckling under intimidation, harassment, or oppression does not mean you are humble.

Humility is a disposition to serve rather than boss others including those below. Humility is being rich and yet mixing freely with the poor. Humility is rulership that does not distance itself from the commoners but treats everyone with respect.

God's plan for you is to situate you above, not below (Deuteronomy

28:13). You are meant to be the head, not the tail. You are meant to reign and exercise dominion. God has indeed made you a king and priest, and you will reign on earth (Revelation 5:10). You must never accept any inferior position as your final stop. Mediocrity or inferiority is not your destiny. You ought not forever be treated as a slave. It is grievous and shocking to see servants on horses while princes are walking (Ecclesiastes 10:7).

In the place of your divine assignment, see yourself in charge. In God's scheme of things, when the righteous are in power, the people rejoice. You must lead by service and deliver value. Demons have no right to rule over you and keep you in bondage. God's Word is clear—He has given you power over the enemy (Luke 10:19). Sickness should not rule over you. Witch doctors should not control or manipulate you. You must rearrange your life and take charge spiritually. You can do this only on your knees before your Maker. You are a royal priest. You are part of a holy nation. You are a believer. Exercise the believer's authority. You are a king, and kings reign. Take back your staff of office.

I see you reigning again. Our God reigns. His children reign with Him.

Anywhere I find myself, I expect to lead somehow. From my earliest days in school, I was always spotted by teachers and seniors. At various posts in my working life and Christian ministry, the mantle of leadership has always fallen on me. It is something I could never quite understand until God explained it to me. He chooses leaders even before they are born. There are always situations that require servant leaders. You too have been chosen to lead by service, so expect to lead and reign. Prepare for leadership by serving God's Word faithfully. Believers are meant to be above, never beneath. He will work it out for you if you serve Him; He has a plan for you.

The Prayer Solution

- I refuse from today to settle for an inferior position as my lot in life in Jesus's name.
- I receive the power to reign over my circumstances from today on in Jesus's name.

- Every usurper of my God-assigned throne be dethroned now in Jesus's name.
- Father, wherever I find myself, help me lead by service and good example in Jesus's name.
- Every position of leadership stolen from me I recover now, and I reclaim my throne in Jesus's name.
- Father, lift me up with the right hand of your righteousness in Jesus's name.

Living on the Mountaintop

Challenges

- When you want to take charge.
- When there is a leadership void you are unable to fill.
- When you are unjustly subordinated or marginalized.
- When you desire to rise to the peak of your career or profession.

The Word Solution

You are meant to lead, direct, and influence matters and people. That is why the Lord Jesus calls you and every one of His disciples the light of the world (Matthew 5:14). His Word is clear—no one should hide a lit candle under a basket; it should be set in a candlestick (Matthew 5:15). Jesus declared that because we were the light of the world, we were a "city set on a hill" (Matthew 5:14). Wherever you find yourself, the mantle of leadership falls on you supernaturally.

There is only one condition necessary for a mountaintop life—obedience to God (Deuteronomy 28:13). If you do what God says you should do, God will do for you what He promised He would. There is no shortcut. Joshua's tremendous success was based on this eternal principle. He totally yielded himself to God in the same manner as did his predecessor, Moses, from whom Joshua learned. "As the Lord commanded Moses his servant, so did Moses command Joshua and so did Joshua; he left nothing undone of all that the Lord commanded Moses"

(Joshua 11:15). Joshua is forever a classic study in mission success. He led the Israelites out of the wilderness to the Land of Promise.

Are you leaving undone anything God commanded you? Are you walking in an opposite direction to God's Commandments? The only way you can arrive at the top is by absolute obedience to God. Change your approach today. I see you arriving at the top of your career, marriage, and ministry as you begin to walk in total obedience.

The Prayer Solution

- From obscurity, Father, announce me to my community and to the whole world in Jesus's name.
- Father, may your mantle of leadership fall on me in Jesus's name.
- I receive the grace and anointing to be above only in Jesus's name.
- Father, help me to live in holiness all the days of my life in Jesus's name.
- Father, lead me to mountaintop living for the rest of my life in Jesus's name.

Seeing the Future

Challenges

- When you think you are succeeding but in reality you are not.
- When you are uncertain of or fretful and frightened about tomorrow.
- When your life seems to be going in circles.
- When you really do not know where you are headed.
- When you have nothing to show for all your struggles.

The Word Solution

You are likely to forget some of what you hear and read, but it is unlikely that you will forget what you see. There is great power in seeing or envisioning. What you see drives you. What you see propels you. What you see creates energy or passion in you.

Visuals whether physical or spiritual paint pictures in our minds. When we see a picture of tomorrow, it gives us an idea of our destination. When we get there, we will know we have arrived. God showed Joseph a picture of his future—he would be promoted and his brothers would one day bow before him. Thirteen years later, that happened. That dream was a divine window that gave Joseph a peek into the future (Genesis 42:9).

Visions are so important because they play a significant role in God's arrangement for the last days (which started from the days of Acts of the Apostles). God spoke to His people through visions and dreams (Joel 2:28; Acts 2:17). He will paint and show you a clear picture of tomorrow.

What do you envision about yourself? Where do you see yourself next year? Where do you see your marriage and household in twenty years? Will you be making desperate provisions for divorce or separation, or will you be enjoying a blissful marriage worth all your pains and sacrifices? Do you see yourself seated beside your spouse aging well and happily playing with your grandchildren? Or you are busy making personal investments behind your spouse's back in readiness for a foreseeable breakdown of your marriage? What do you really see in your mind?

How about your business? Do you see it expanding tenfold in five years? Most things I have accomplished or received in life were first shown to me in dreams or visions. In some cases, I was forewarned against sharing the received revelation with anyone. They were all fulfilled as I obeyed the leading of the Spirit and walked in faith.

Ten years before I was ordained a pastor, God showed me in a dream an image of myself standing at a pulpit and preaching to a large congregation. But at that time, I was not even a committed member of a church. Nonetheless, God brought the dream to pass in His own way and time.

Many people fail to prosper because they are unable to see tomorrow. Many are so tied up with the present or so deeply trapped in the past that they have no time to think of tomorrow much less envision or dream about it. Most people are just going through the motions of daily; they think success is an accident. Are you one of those?

Any archer will tell you that missing the mark is a natural consequence of failing to aim well. Success is not a matter of chance; it takes planning and aiming at clear goals and objectives. It takes strong envisioning. You must set yourself a target and benchmark or every mediocre score would seem to you like a great success. Where there is no vision, people perish (Proverbs 29:18).

Do you have a guiding vision? Make sure to write it down. Right now. Write it in a special notebook, a book that you must keep handy for regular meditation. Keep looking at the written vision, and assess your progress toward it from time to time. Every believer would find this divine challenge highly motivational and beneficial. You must write the vision down and then run with it (Habakkuk 2:2–3).

Stop going through fruitless motions. Plan for tomorrow, envision your tomorrow, and let that vision drive you. Work toward it. You will get there with the help of God.

The Prayer Solution

- Father, open my eyes to see the future in Jesus's name.
- Father, please remove all demonic veils blocking my spiritual eyes in Jesus's name.
- Father, help me dream big dreams in Jesus's name.
- Father, help me set targets, work toward them, and achieve them.
- Father, speak to me through visions and dreams regularly in Jesus's name.
- Father, remind me of every important dream I have forgotten in Jesus's name.
- Father, give me the wisdom to do what I must do for my dreams to be realized in Jesus's name.

Divine Honor

Challenges

- When you want to be celebrated.
- When you desire a place in the front seat.
- When you wish to come out of obscurity and join the big leagues.

The Word Solution

People generally strive hard to be recognized and honored by others. We like to be appreciated and held in honor. In Africa for example, people who contribute substantially to the development of their communities expect to be rewarded with, say, chieftaincy titles. Monarchies such as England celebrate major achievers by conferring knighthood, lordship, or other titles on them. Other nations reward outstanding services by conferring national honors and awards. Many leading cities honor distinguished friends with keys to the city, an emblem of full rights of permanent residency.

But God's honor is different; we do not earn it by exceptional works or winning tournament championships. God brings His chosen to honor. He takes those who have achieved nothing in this world and exalts them to great honor as he did David, a shepherd boy, and Joseph, whom his brothers had sold into slavery. God honored Mordecai, a prisoner in Babylon, by replacing Hamman with Mordecai. God is an expert when it comes to honoring those the world despises. Once God honors someone, all others must do so as well.

One Sunday, I needed to catch the last flight home after a preaching engagement to be back at my office on Monday morning. Unfortunately, I arrived at the airport an hour after check-in had closed, but my plane was still there; no one at the counter, however, could tell what was going on.

On fervent persuasion, they reluctantly sold me a ticket and told me to try my luck. My testimony to the glory of God is that I got onboard, and just as I sat down, the pilot was heard ordering the door to be shut. He apologized to the grumbling passengers for the long delay in taking off, but he did not offer any reason for the delay. I later heard from other passengers that they had waited for over forty-five minutes with no explanations by the crew; everyone had surmised that the wait was for an unnamed VIP. Friend, with all due sense of humility, I was the VIP. If you work for Jesus, you are His ambassador. God can do anything for those who work for Him.

Divine honor is superior to human honor. To receive divine honor, you must be humble (Proverbs 15:33). You must honor God for Him to honor you (1 Samuel 2:30). The way to honor God is to fear Him by putting Him first and obeying His Word. He honors those who fear Him (Psalm 15:4).

God wants to honor men and women. Fear Him, humble yourself, honor Him, and expect divine honor in return.

The Prayer Solution

- Father, honor me by yourself in Jesus's name.
- Father, position me for useful service in Jesus's name.
- Father, elevate me to your glory and make it permanent in Jesus's name.
- Father, teach me to humble myself and gain your honor in Jesus's name.
- Father, because I reverence you, glorify yourself in me in Jesus's name.
- Father, may I not lose the honor you bestowed on me in Jesus's name.

Uncommon Favor

Challenges

- When you labor so much but have very little to show for your efforts.
- When you need to be chosen among your peers or competitors.
- When you need a divine push to make it.
- When your rating is below the eligibility criteria for the next level.

The Word Solution

When close friends or relations come to your aid, that is common favor. By their very nature, friendship and family ties engender mutual support, so giving and receiving favor in such cases is expected. Sometimes, human favor is only payback for favor received or an outlay for an anticipated favor. Common favor is therefore invariably based on a material or emotional consideration. Because it flows from fellow human beings, it is limited, imperfect, and hardly ever fully satisfying. People will rarely favor you without demanding something in return.

But then there is uncommon favor. It comes from God. It is a game changer without which no one can excel or realize his or her fullest potential. Even the Lord Jesus in His earthly walk needed favor from His Father. We read that in His adolescence, He "increased with favor from both man and God" (Luke 2:52). In the same manner, the young Samuel growing up in the house of the Lord enjoyed favor from man and God (1 Samuel 2:26).

God's favor may be yours undeservedly, but to enjoy it in full and for all time, you must give yourself up to righteous living (Psalm 5:12). The quest for championship comes with plenty of struggles and workouts. Have you been working hard to become wealthy? Have you been frantically searching for a treasured thing, a life partner for example? Have you labored hard but have not received reward for your efforts? You need uncommon favor, the help that only God can give. Uncommon favor makes up for all your deficiencies no matter how great. When I registered as a freshman at university in 1980, I was among the smallest and youngest in a long and exhausting queue of students waiting to register and receive a hostel accommodation. The schedule staffers were weary and about to shut down for the day when an elderly woman officer left her desk and walked straight to me at the end of the queue. She took my documents, registered me, and gave me a hostel accommodation. That was God's uncommon favor at work.

Uncommon favor qualifies you when you are not humanly qualified. It opens doors for you and gives you access to royalty (Esther 5:1–3). It distinguishes you and clearly makes you preferred above others (Daniel 1:19). When God's uncommon favor is working for you, no enemy can ever defeat you (Psalm 41:11).

What are you waiting for? Ask God to clothe you with uncommon favor starting today.

The Prayer Solution

- Father, may your uncommon favor cause me to rise above my weaknesses in Jesus's name.
- Please cover and blot out every deficiency or disadvantage in my family with your favor in Jesus's name.
- Father, I have heard about divine favor; let me begin to experience it today in Jesus's name.
- Father, let me grow in your favor every day in Jesus's name.
- Father, let me enjoy favor before others in Jesus's name.
- Father, separate me from whatever could cost me your favor in Jesus's name.
- Father, let me be a permanent vessel of your favor in Jesus's name.

Capturing Opportunities

Challenges

- When you desire a significant lifting up.
- When you want to see a new and better dawn.
- When you want to change old ways of doing things.

The Word Solution

There is a lot to learn from these two real-life stories. The first concerns a pastor in East Africa whose periodic open-air services were big media events that abounded with miracles and public testimonies. A regular guest minister and key preacher at these massively advertised services was his American associate, a crowd-pulling great name and faith healer.

There came one big occasion that had been heavily advertised, but the popular American preacher who was billed to be there called to cancel his appearance. His distraught African host rose to the occasion and faced the unbelievable crowd alone. To his utter amazement, what followed was a catalogue of astounding miracles that turned him into a widely sought-after healing minister from that day on.

The second relates to yours truly, who some twenty years ago was working in a city. My friend, a fellow banker, was abruptly summoned to corporate headquarters for an emergency meeting. He implored me to stand in for him at a training program for which he had been engaged as a facilitator by a high-profile training and consultancy firm. That was unfamiliar ground for me; I had never done that sort of gig, and the consulting firm knew nothing of me and was naturally skeptical about the quick change of personnel. They reluctantly allowed me to proceed, however, and the result of that session has been simply amazing. I became their regular facilitator for the next twenty years and became program director there on a part-time basis. I am still serving the firm as a consultant.

The two stories above illustrate divinely arranged opportunities that open the door of uncommon favor. In Potiphar's house, Joseph was a mere houseboy, but he saw an opportunity to shine and grabbed it with both hands. He could well have chosen a life of hate and bitterness forever fuming at the wickedness of his envious brothers who had so inhumanely sold him into slavery. Instead, he refused to allow that awful, devastating experience to define the rest of his life. The result of such a winning attitude was that he excelled in relations with people and in the performance of his duties to the point that Potiphar entrusted his entire household to him (Genesis. 39:6).

Joseph maintained that forgiving attitude even after he was unjustly thrown into prison on a false charge of attempted rape. His unbowed spirit of excellence won him the respect of the prison superintendent, who entrusted him with the welfare of the other prisoners (Genesis 39:22). During his prison ministry, he interpreted dreams for an inmate, a routine service that eventually catapulted him to the palace.

God noted David, a shepherd boy, as someone with great courage, and He gave David the power and opportunity to slay Goliath—a God-given opportunity to excel. David's feat launched him into immediate stardom. Women composed songs about his heroism, and the king enlisted him in his palace retinue. Soon, David's prodigious talent as singer and harpist was on display. His journey to kingship had started.

How many opportunities that came your way have you wasted? Opportunities never announce themselves; they come mostly in the form of challenges or problems.

The Lord Jesus stated that those who were faithful in little things would be faithful in much more (Luke 16:10). Be faithful, therefore, in your conduct and service wherever you are. Every contact you make and every service you render might turn out to be a stepping stone to your destiny. From now on, take no assignment lightly. God is watching. People are watching too. God is setting you up for honor, not failure. Be sensitive. Recognize and capture what opportunities come your way.

Be good to people. Excel in your job. Destiny is calling. Soon and very soon, I will hear your testimonies in Jesus's name.

The Prayer Solution

- Father, open my eyes to recognize opportunities for promotion when they arise.
- Father, forgive me for wasting past opportunities.
- Father, connect me to the right people, places, and circumstances for useful service and recognition.
- Father, disconnect me from time-wasting pursuits and indolence.
- Father, help me be faithful in every situation.
- Father, enable me to take responsibility as a vessel of honor for service to you and to people in every situation.
- Father, enable me to regain every lost opportunity in Jesus's name.

Chapter 4

Restoration Capsules

Rise Up and Move

Challenges

- When you have lost a lot and you desperately need divine restoration.
- When all hopes appear lost and you don't know what to do.
- When you are down and unable to find your feet.
- When enemies are mocking you because though you were once a clear success, you have become a seeming failure.

The Word Solution

Anyone can be knocked down by the vagaries of life. Financial challenges can bring a person down. So can sickness, business failures, marital problems, career setbacks, family troubles, and the like. No human enterprise is immune to disappointment, drawback, defeat, destruction, or death. The Lord Jesus admonished us that in this world, tribulations are sure to come (John 16:33) just as persecutions are inevitable (John 15:20). The Bible refers to this as the troubles of the present time (Romans 8:18).

The good news is that God wants us to rise above our challenges and has equipped us to overcome them. Even when we suffer momentary setbacks, we ought to keep in mind that such a downturn does not mean our end. Micah warned his enemies not to mock him when he was down; he was confident that he would rise again (Micah 7:8–10). God's Word proclaims that we, his children, are more than conquerors (Romans 8:37). We must never accept our fallen state as a permanent and irremediable condition.

"Arise and shine for your time has come" (Isaiah 60:1). You are not meant to be consigned to the dust while there is still breath in you. Rise like the eagle you are and soar to the heights that are meant for you. You are meant to be above only (Deuteronomy 28:13). Recognize who you are—royalty because your Father is the King.

I have in my career lost a couple of jobs. Each time it happened, I felt challenged to secure a better one, and in all cases, the new jobs I got turned out far better, more fulfilling, and more rewarding than the ones I lost. I learned to stay upbeat and never give up.

Restoration is of God. You win it on your knees with eyes and heart lifted to God. Remember Job. What he lost, he got back twice over (Job 42:10).

You are a royal priesthood. You are meant to rule. Rise up and rule. Assert your authority over your circumstances and call on the Lord Jesus; heaven will back you up.

The Prayer Solution

- I tell anyone laughing at my fallen state that I will rise again in Jesus's name.
- Father, God of second chances, give me another start in Jesus's name.
- Father, I do not want to remain down; lift me up in Jesus's name.
- Father, turn my failure into success in Jesus's name.
- I refuse to be down and out; Father, raise me and keep me above in Jesus's name.
- Father, give me the grace to overcome every trial and tribulation in Jesus's name.
- Father, convert my challenges into opportunities in Jesus's name.

Overcoming Losses

Challenges

- When you desire to overcome your losses.
- When you desire to recover from setbacks.
- When you face business failure, drastic loss of income, or diminution of assets.
- When you lose your job.
- When you suffer an irrecoverable loss, e.g., the death of a loved one.

The Word Solution

Accounting and bookkeeping practices include keeping a profit and loss account, the bottom line. Nothing but profit can reverse losses. The great apostle Paul testified that though he had lost all things, he counted it but gain for Christ (Philippians 3:7–8). As far as he was concerned, gaining Jesus was profit that compensated for the losses he had incurred. He was left with a net profit and the dividends that came with it.

What have you lost because of the kingdom of Christ? The Lord promises anyone who loses land, houses, money, or family for the kingdom that he or she will receive a hundredfold payback (Mark 10:29–30).

One of Jesus's many parables related to sowing seed and reaping a harvest (Luke 6:38). God can grant full compensation for whatever losses you might have suffered in previous seasons through greater harvests in the future. He is the God of restoration; He is able and willing to compensate for years of famine (Joel 2:23–25). God can redeem anything, including time. I know of a couple who endured long years of childlessness but were blessed with twins—repeatedly.

Are you still worried about any earthly loss you suffered for the sake of your faith in God? Our God is a God of profit. A single business transaction with Him could compensate for heavy past losses. Weeping may endure for a night, but joy comes in the morning (Psalm 30:5). You may have gone out sowing in tears, but you will come back with a joyful harvest (Psalm 126:6).

The Prayer Solution

- Father, profit my business and cancel out all previous losses in Jesus's name.
- Restore sevenfold whatever the enemy has stolen from me, Father, in Jesus's name.
- Revive everything the enemy has destroyed in my life, Father, in Jesus's name.
- Father, send me the former and latter rain in right season in Jesus's name.

Total Recovery

Challenges

- When you desire recovery of all you have lost.
- When you need to overpower robbers of your God-given resources.
- When you need divine restoration in every aspect of your life.

The Word Solution

Recovery is the process of taking back what has been stolen, lost, or damaged. Even a human being can be recovered—reclaimed from captivity. An example is David, who recovered his wives and children (1 Samuel 30:18–19).

Health can also be recovered. One ready biblical illustration is the case of Naaman, the Syrian general who recovered from leprosy (2 Kings 5:6) by obeying the word of Elisha that he had initially almost disregarded.

Lost opportunities can be difficult to recover, but with God, nothing is impossible. He can send rain that produces plenty. He knows how to restore and whom to compensate (Joel 2:34–25).

I do not know what you have lost, but God said we would recover all we have lost. It is not your business to know how He does it; God cannot be taught by anyone.

Play your own part—cry out to Him in fervent prayer and seek His face as David did when he had lost all he had and you will recover all as he did (1 Samuel 30:18–19). Job is another man who lost all he had. The scriptures bear witness that when Job prayed for his friends, God turned around his captivity and he recovered everything he had lost (Job 42:10).

Press on through prayer now for yourself and for your friends. You can surely recover all you have lost. But do not forget to tell God what you will do with all you recover. It's a deal, and you will see God's faithfulness.

The Prayer Solution

- I will recover all the enemy has stolen from me in Jesus's name.
- Grant me recovery of every damage I have suffered, Father, in Jesus's name.
- Father, grant me full recovery from any bodily infirmity in Jesus's name.
- Father, restore every good opportunity I have lost in Jesus's name.
- I command a sevenfold recovery of whatever the enemy has stolen from me in Jesus's name.
- I pursue, overtake, and recover all I have lost in Jesus's name.

Uncommon Recoveries

Challenges

- When you want recovery of stolen, lost, or impaired virtues.
- When you desire recovery that seems impossible.
- When you want God's help for an unusual restoration.

The Word Solution

Sometimes when thieves are caught, what they stole is returned. The Amalekites who attacked David's camp carried away his wives and children, but David pursued them and recovered all they had stolen (Isaiah 30:18).

Our God is an expert in handling any situation no matter how hopeless it seems. The Lord Jesus is a miracle worker. He is Lord, the author of life and master of uncommon recoveries. Had not Lazarus been dead and buried for four days? His case was seemingly beyond hope. Mary reproached him for turning up late; she said that had He arrived while her brother was only sick, he would not have died (John 11:32). Jesus wrought an uncommon recovery of Lazarus's life.

The sons of the prophets borrowed an axe-head to cut wood on the banks of the Jordan River. To the consternation of the young men, it fell into the river and could not be found. The prophet Elisha tossed a piece of wood into the river, and the axe-head floated (2 Kings 6:1–7). That was God's hand working out an uncommon recovery.

I once missed out on a due and expected promotion. A year after, another promotion exercise took place. For everyone but me on that list, the effective date was as per the release date on the staff notice, but my promotion was backdated one year to the date of my previously missed promotion and I was paid one year's salary in arrears. That uncommon recovery was God at work. God says that hopeless cases will be reversed and losses will turn into gains.

I see contracts that were previously canceled now being again awarded. I see laid-off staff being recalled and several of them gaining promotions. I see debts being canceled and forgiven in favor of God's children. I see so-called terminal illnesses being healed. At the same time, I see your debtors turning up to pay the debts they owe you, some that you had written off.

Position yourself for uncommon recoveries. Losses of past years are about to be wiped out. Earnings are coming from unexpected sources.

The Prayer Solution

- Please return to me sevenfold all that the enemy has stolen from me, Father, in Jesus's name.
- Reverse every hopeless case in my life, Father, in Jesus's name.
- Resurrect every good thing the enemy has stolen from my family, Father, in Jesus's name.

- Reverse whatever is plotted in the enemy's camp against me and mine, Father, by your mercy and power in Jesus's name.
- Reverse curses that men consider irreversible, Father, in Jesus's name.
- Heal any manner of sickness in my family, Father, in Jesus's name.
- Restore every good thing I have given up on, Father, in Jesus's name.

The Return of God's Glory

Challenges

- When you want a return of God's presence in your life.
- When you desire spiritual gifts to come alive again in your life.
- When you want all shame to be turned to glory.

The Word Solution

Glory and honor are in God's presence (1 Chronicles 16:27). God's glory and presence determine events and outcomes in favor of His people.

An example was Paul and Silas (Acts 16:25) in prison chains but nonetheless praying and singing praises to God. They were delivered when God's glory descended on the jailhouse and caused an earthquake that loosened their chains and threw the doors open.

Equally unforgettable was the pillar of fire that guided, warmed, and protected God's people in the desert. God's manifest presence is glorious, and all His glory redounds to the defense and protection of His people (Isaiah 4:4–5).

When God's glory departs, problems arise. When the Israelites offended God, His glory departed (1 Samuel 4:21), and the immediate consequence was the sudden deaths of Eli, the high priest, and his errant sons Hophni and Phinehas. Some people have lost God's glory. There are even churches from which God's glory has departed. Some families that used to experience His glory are no longer walking in His presence.

The good news is that God's glory can still return. It takes only a sinner's genuine repentance for God's mercy to turn up and usher in right in the return of His glory. Ask for His mercy, and His glory will return with it. The voices of the bride and bridegroom will be heard again in your family, the voices of rejoicing and gladness. The enemy who taunted you will be put on the run. Your hair that the enemy had shaved off will grow again as Samson's did. God's glory will return to your church, and yours will be the testimony of quickened answer to prayers.

Some years ago, I pastored an ailing church. Early on there, I felt that God's glory had left that troubled congregation. The few who had jobs were losing them, young men were dying in numbers, and too many people were becoming sick. Weddings and childbirth were rare events, and church services were attended by a dwindling number. Even I, the pastor, was living from hand to mouth.

I thanked God for intercessors, the mighty few we call prayer warriors, who knew what it meant to stand in the gap. They and I sought the face of God, and He began to reveal that the enemy had taken up residence in the church through his human agents of spiritual wickedness by whose connivance he was killing, stealing, and destroying at will.

We raised the spiritual temperature of the church through prayers and fasting. After one year, the agents of Satan began to leave one by one. The glory of the Lord returned ushering in testimonies of new jobs for the unemployed, including me, and childbirths by the score. Houses and cars were being dedicated again, and weddings and baby showers were back. In no time, we were enlarging the church building as membership had increased threefold.

When God's glory returns to your marriage, peace will return and marital crises will be brought to an end. When the glory returns, your business will flourish again.

Friend, pray fervently for the return of His glory.

The Prayer Solution

- Father, never let your glory depart from me again in Jesus's name.
- Father, let your glory envelop my family forever in Jesus's name.
- Father, may I never again do anything that will cost me your glory in Jesus's name.

- Father, may the glory ahead be far greater than what I've seen thus far in Jesus's name.
- Father, let your glory be the sole defense of my family in Jesus's name.
- Father, let there be visible evidence of your glory in my family in Jesus's name.
- Father, from now on, let your glory guide me and lead me in Jesus's name.

Power of Prophetic Pronouncements

Challenges

- When you are in a dire situation.
- When you come under siege and feel fear on every side.
- When you are so drained that you cannot even pray for yourself.
- When you have prayed all you can but have received no answer.
- When you are overwhelmed and desire a quick turnaround.

The Word Solution

Most times when children of God are faced with tough situations, their instant resort is to traditional solutions or routines. The commonest is to rush into prayers and possibly observe some days of fasting to complement the exercise. With daytime prayers and midnight cries intensified, we bombard the heavens with fervent expectation that God's answer will come quickly. It is an approach that is quite in order and produces results most of the time.

But there are times that no matter how fervent our personal exertions are, no change might seem forthcoming. Are you in that situation at present? Have you considered a change in approach? Instead of battling alone, why don't you approach your pastor to pray and make emphatic declarations over your life? Do you know that one minute of prophetic declaration by your spiritual cover can be more powerful than weeks of lone prayers and vigils? The efficacy of a prophetic pronouncement of a true servant of God is profound. A man of God is an extension of the hand of God; his voice is an extension of the voice of God. He is in your life to bless you. He is there as God's general with power to restrain the devil from interfering with you. At His word of blessing over you, God causes events that bring your prayers to fruition.

Consider the Syrian siege of Samaria (2 Kings 6–7). Famine brought the beleaguered people to the point of cannibalism with their supply lines cut off. Caught between the two disastrous options of capitulating unconditionally or starving to death, the people must have cried out to God in prayers until their last ounce of strength. Theirs was not a spiritual fast; it was imposed starvation. They were in no position to think about putting up praise sessions.

As hopeless as their situation was, it was turned around dramatically and rapidly. A man of God simply made a statement that in twenty-four hours, there would be a turnaround and abundance would reign in the city (2 Kings 7:1). The moment Elisha made that statement, there was an instant change in the spiritual climate, and the womb of time was set to birth the declaration God's servant had made on His behalf. Four lepers starved beyond caring for life suddenly began to move out of their hiding place just outside the city gates. They were headed for the Syrian camp in desperation, and God made their shuffling walk sound like chariots; the Syrians fled in panic leaving their vast supplies. The lepers fed to the full. Samaria had abundance; the word of the prophet was fulfilled to the letter.

When last did you request your pastor to pronounce a blessing over your life? When he made those prophetic declarations, did you really believe and receive them in faith? Did you notice that a certain officer doubted Elisha? He died as a consequence of that; he was the only person not to benefit from the promised abundance. God's Word is firm on that point: "Believe in the Lord your God, so shall you be established; believe His prophets, so shall you prosper" (2 Chronicles 20:20).

In one Holy Spirit service, Pastor E. A. Adeboye declared prophetically that the dry season was over for someone. He advised the person to let himself be thoroughly drenched by the next rainfall as a sign that the drought was over. I relayed that instruction to all my parishioners, and

I obeyed it myself. A few hours after my drenching in the rain, I got a phone call offering me a lucrative job.

You have prayed well enough for yourself and maybe fasted for too long as well. You may have to change your approach and open up to the man of God He placed as shepherd over you. Ask him to pray for you and make a pronouncement over your life.

I see you running to your pastor to testify about answered prayer. God honors His faithful servants.

The Prayer Solution

- Father, put in the mouth of a man of God a word of blessing for my benefit in Jesus's name.
- Father, anoint me to pronounce prophetic blessings on your people in Jesus's name.
- Manifest every beneficial prophecy over my destiny now in Jesus's name.
- Father, connect me to your worthy servants you empower to make prophetic declarations over my life in Jesus's name.
- Begin to manifest every prophetic pronouncement I have made over myself and my family in Jesus's name.

Chapter 5

Prosperity Capsules

The Sound of Abundance

Challenges

- When poverty and lack have held you down for too long and you need a change.
- When scarcity and drought seem to be permanent features of your life.
- When there seems no sign or hope of prosperity.

The Word Solution

For three years, there was severe drought in Israel, a direct consequence of a whole generation's widespread idol worship. God's anger had been kindled against the people and their fetish king, Ahab, causing the dire prophetic utterance of the prophet Elijah (1 Kings 17:1).

By God's leading, Elijah encountered the prophets of Baal on Mount Carmel on a day of reckoning. Elijah began by repairing God's altar and offering a sacrifice on it to Him. When he called on God, fire fell from heaven. The prophets of Baal were disgraced and put to the sword. Elijah thereafter announced what he called an "abundance of rain" (1 Kings 18:41). Not long after came the long-awaited and much sought-after rainfall. The drought was over.

Our times are no different. As in the days of Elijah, sin still hinders the rain of divine mercies. It still prolongs the dry season that troubles many lives. The long drought is not God's plan for you; it must be brought to a quick end. Drought must cease in your finances, marriage, ministry, and family. Can you hear the sound of abundance of rain? It speaks of bountiful blessings and fantastic breakthroughs and breakouts.

All you need is to repair the altar of God in your family. Follow the example set by the prophet Elijah. Repair your family altar and rededicate it to God in prayer. Attend to this emergency with urgency. Reconcile with God without delay. He is ever faithful and will reunite you to Himself and restore you to His blessings out of all seasons.

A few months after I had given my life to Jesus Christ, I fell into sin. Recognizing that I had offended God, I cried all night feeling I was on my way to hell. I was bitterly disappointed with myself. In remorse, I confessed my misdeed to the woman who had led me to Jesus and sought her prayers. I was sure God would slay me that night in spite of her spirited assurances to the contrary.

That night, I had a vision in which I was shown a scriptural verse, Micah 7:18, and waking up, I read it: "Who is a God like unto thee that pardoneth iniquity and passeth by the transgressions of the remnant of his heritage? He retaineth not his anger forever because he delighted in mercy." Friend, this scripture strengthened me. I felt forgiven. I had received mercy, and I felt restored in fellowship with God.

Right after that, my spiritual gifts began to manifest again. The dry season had given way to rain in abundance, and all facets of my life were blossoming again. That was some twenty years ago. I made a vow never again to consciously offend my God. It has been a wonderful covenant that He has very faithfully enabled me to keep.

Your blessings are set to pour down like rain. I hear abundant rain. Welcome to uncommon grace and favor. Get ready for a downpour of divine blessings.

The Prayer Solution

- Father, give me the grace to repair my family's broken altar in Jesus's name.
- Father, turn my lacks and insufficiencies into blessed overabundance in Jesus's name.
- Father, guide me to guide others into abundant life from today in Jesus's name.
- Father, may my family and I begin to hear the sound of abundance of rain in Jesus's name.
- Whatever is delaying my harvest time, Father, terminate in Jesus's name.

Overcoming Poverty

Challenges

- When you are tired of the chains and pains of poverty.
- When you desperately wish to conquer and be done with poverty.
- When you desire to prosper in a sinless way.
- When you seek to know the secrets of genuine wealth.

The Word Solution

Poverty is a terrible curse. It is an evil force wreaking havoc on lives and homes. Poverty robs people of confidence and self-esteem. It aborts dreams and ambitions. It has caused many an intelligent child to drop out of school. It is the scourge behind thousands of epidemics and millions of premature deaths. Countless numbers die every day from preventable and curable diseases simply because they cannot afford the treatment. Poverty destroys social and moral values. It fuels corruption and breeds inequality that often results in hate, crime, and violence.

The good news is that you do not have to remain poor. God, who made you, is not happy with poverty. That is why the Lord Jesus said that He came to give us life and to give it to us more abundantly (John 10:10). God wants His children to prosper and be in good health (3 John 1:2).

Our loving Father takes pleasure in the prosperity of His servants (Psalm 35:27). We have assurance in His Word that wealth and riches will be in the house of the righteous (Psalm 112:3). God says the righteous will not borrow but will instead be lenders to many nations (Deuteronomy 28:12).

You will indeed become wealthy. All you need to do is play by the scriptural rules and avoid committing the sins of the desperate people who seek riches without conscience and fear of God. Such people are readily manipulated by Satan; they are blinded by the lure and attraction of deceptive riches, and they fall into death pits in their blind haste.

God's given riches are so different; they bring you no sorrow (Proverbs 10:22). God's principles for acquiring wealth are straightforward. Unfortunately, most Christians are more inclined to follow their own routines than heed God's stated principles for getting rich. They would rather pray and fast for months and years to be made rich than simply accept God's simple key to manifold riches. Our Lord Jesus laid it all out (Luke 6:38); God commanded us to give in order to get back in overflowing measure. We must sow seed in tears to reap a harvest in rejoicing (Psalm 126:5–6).

We reap whatever we sow (Galatians 6:7). Prosperity is anchored on the principle of seed and harvest as laid down forever in God's covenant with Noah. It is the principle of giving and receiving, and the payback is always a huge multiple of the outlay. It is the investment principle—giving in the present to receive a future greater yield. It is the fundamental truth of spiritual maturity, a sacrifice today for God's blessings tomorrow, an offering up of the visible and tangible for what is hoped and prayed for. That was the crucial testing ground for Abraham when God demanded that he sacrificially give up his beloved son, the precious child of promise that God gave him only after several decades of a trying wait. After Abraham proved his sacrificial disposition, God kept His promise to him by giving him children as numberless as the stars (Genesis 22:16–18). God Himself gave up His only begotten Son that He may thereby reap the harvest of all humankind (John 3:16).

If you want to prosper, sow seeds; that is a precondition. You must give up what you have before you can receive what you wish for. The God of creation will multiply and return bountifully to you whatever you sacrificially release.

God's kingdom is a fertile ground for your faith sowing. Sow sacrificially in the work of the kingdom and earn a hundredfold return (Mark 10:29–30). God's promise awaits you as you bring your tithes and offerings; He will open the windows of heaven for you (Malachi 3:10).

I have a personal testimony on this aspect of God's abiding grace, something that happened years ago—I sowed my 5 kv generator to the church, and not long after, someone gave me a 27 kv generator. Doesn't that remind you of King Solomon? He gave sacrificially to God, and God made him extraordinarily wealthy. The giver's hand is always on top.

Get done with tightfistedness—open your hands and scatter your seed because you do not know who will prosper from it (Ecclesiastes 11:6). Give liberally because a liberal soul will be made fat (Proverbs 11:25). Give bountifully and reap bountifully (2 Corinthians 9:6). Stop holding back. Test your God; challenge Him with your sacrificial seed and see whether He will not prosper you with a joyful harvest. He will give you power to create wealth (Deuteronomy 8:18).

God will make you rich if you follow His principles, not those of the world. The world says, "Keep it and become rich," but God is saying, "Give it to me and I will multiply it for you." Be smart—do it God's way.

I see poverty fleeing from you today as you begin a new life of sowing in God's kingdom.

The Prayer Solution

- Father, guide me in giving right to overcome poverty in Jesus's name.
- Father, give me grace to invest wisely always in Jesus's name.
- Father, show and deliver me from habits and attitudes that keep me in poverty in Jesus's name.
- In the name of Jesus, I break every curse of poverty operating in my family. I receive for my family the blessings of God that make us rich and add no sorrow in Jesus's name.
- Father, bless every work of my hands and cause me to prosper in Jesus's name.
- Father, enable me to be a great sower in your kingdom in Jesus's name.
- I reject every agent of poverty in my life in Jesus's name.

Breaking into Prosperity

Challenges

- When you are yearning for a prosperity breakthrough.
- When you are tired of begging others for help.
- When you are beginning to imagine that you will never be rich in this life.
- When your labors are beset with disappointments and frustrations.
- When you are determined to overcome all obstacles and prosper mightily.
- When you are facing a serious discouragement in your bid to prosper.

The Word Solution

The Bible views prosperity as an all-round package of wealth, good health, and wholesomeness of soul (3 John 1:2). Contrary to some misleading theologies, God wants us all to prosper. God takes pleasure in the prosperity of His servants (Psalm 35:27). God intends good health for all His children as well. His promise on that is explicit: He would take away the diseases of the Egyptians from us (Exodus 15:26). He wants us to gain heaven too; He sent His Son so our souls would gain eternal life (John 3:16).

Seeking prosperity requires honest effort. You must work hard, be resilient, and never give up. Isaac kept digging for water but kept meeting obstacles; the enemy seized one after another of two wells he dug, but he did not give up. He went to another place and dug again until he struck water, and there was no further contention (Genesis 26:26–33). That was his breakthrough.

You must stay on it and not give up. Those who give up never achieve the breakthrough they need. You must keep giving of yourself to your business and sow all the time into God's work as well. Keep searching for that job. Keep tendering for those contracts. Keep working in that office. Keep staying in the Word and living a holy life so your soul will prosper. Those who endure to the end will be saved (Matthew 24:13).

Keep confessing the Word of God over your life. Keep praising God for your good health and breakthrough. Keep thanking God for your marriage even if it has yet to happen. Keep praising God for your children and the babies you are expecting. Just keep at it; you will get it. Do not become discouraged. Your faith is being tested. It is not over until you get what you need. Do not fail on the very cusp of your miracle. Never consider quitting because quitters never win. That last punch may give you victory over your opponent. That one more attempt may open the door to your breakthrough. Keep believing in and trusting God. Your breakthrough is but one step away.

The Prayer Solution

- Father, prosper me in all ways in Jesus's name.
- Father, expand my coast in Jesus's name.
- Father, open the doors of prosperity for me in Jesus's name.
- Father, usher me into prosperity in Jesus's name.
- Father, remove every limitations to my prosperity in Jesus's name.
- Father, command prosperity to follow me in Jesus's name.
- Father, encourage me and never let me give up my quest to prosper in Jesus's name.

Possessing the Land of Milk and Honey

Challenges

- When you have tarried for too long in the wilderness.
- When you need full reward and rest having labored for years.
- When you want to enter God's rest.
- When you want God to settle you.
- When you want houses you did not build and vineyards you did not plant.

The Word Solution

God describes the Promised Land as a place flowing with milk and honey, a term symbolic of paradise, heaven on earth. It is a land of rest, a land of wealth and prosperity, a place of peace and joy unspeakable. Getting there from Egypt should have taken just forty days of trekking, but it took the Israelites forty years. They suffered in the wilderness, but God sustained them with heavenly bread, manna. They also enjoyed good health throughout their march; no feeble one was among their tribes during that eventful journey (Psalm 105:35). But on arrival in Canaan, they thought they would just take over the land and settle down for some fun and enjoyment. They forgot there were giants in the land (Numbers 13:33).

Friend, every land of promise has its own giants. But that is no reason to see yourself as a grasshopper in their sight (Numbers 13:33). Possessing the land before you is a mission that requires you to obey God completely and never fear those giants. That way, the Lord will delight in you and the giants will become bread for you (Numbers 14:8–9).

What job do you desire? What breakthrough do you hunger for? What quality marriage are you craving? Those are your own Promised Land, your own Canaan. Fear not those occupying the position at this moment. Just live holy and prepare to fight in prayer for your Land of Promise. God told the Israelites that even though He had given them the Promised Land, they would have to contend with the inhabitants (Deuteronomy 2:24). You must fight on your knees in prayer; there is no victory without a fight.

I have interacted with many successful men and women including top ministers of God. They all had one thing in common—they were hard workers and fervent prayers who were determined never to give up. They expected to fight all problems and win no matter how long it took. You cannot attain the highest positions of wealth and success without a godly fight.

The Prayer Solution

- I take authority over and bind every giant in my Canaan in Jesus's name.
- I receive anointing to conquer every opposition to my dreamland in Jesus's name.
- I overcome every source or cause of fear in my life in Jesus's name.
- Father, help me to mount up with wings like an eagle in Jesus's name.
- Father, contend with all who contend with me in battle in Jesus's name.
- I take captive every power or person opposing my entering my Promised Land in Jesus's name.
- Father, open every door shut against my Land of Promise in Jesus's name.

Provoking Divine Release

Challenges

- When you need good things but God doesn't seem interested.
- When you wonder what to do to get God's attention.
- When you are praying but getting no answer from God.

The Word Solution

Every day, we are confronted with our needs and the challenge of how to meet them. Our needs come in varied forms and keep changing. But God knows all our needs even before we bring them to Him in prayer. Yet as a basic principle, He does not impose His help; He waits for those who need His help to ask for it. That is why Jesus exhorted His flock, "Ask and you shall receive" (Matthew 7:7). By implication, if you do not ask, you will not receive. If you expect God to attend to your needs because He knows them all without your speaking, you will get nothing. God simply does not work that way. Blind Bartimaeus made a desperate effort to reach Jesus. Still, the Master asked him what he wanted of Him even though like everyone else, He could see that the man was blind and needed healing (Mark 10:51). Jesus required him to ask.

Another key principle that is guaranteed to provoke divine release is giving and especially to the work of God. Some years ago, my church was building an outstation parish. I committed all my allowances and almost my entire salary to the project. I remember telling the pastor to contact me anytime that church ran out of funds for the project, a crazy call by any standard. The day the general overseer, Pastor Adeboye, dedicated the church, a friend gave me a surprise present of a huge sum of money with the suggestion that I use it to buy some land for myself. In less than six months and with other gifts from friends and well-wishers, I built my first house. Our God is a covenant keeper. He works on His eternal principle of returning to the giver a multiple of his offering (Mark 10:29–30; Luke 6:38; 2 Chronicles 1:1–12).

If you give nothing to God, you will receive nothing from Him. Giving to God moves Him to give back to you. Today, give God an offering through your church. Give especially to any program or project that meets God's needs. Photocopy your sacrificial check, and write on it what you require from God. You will be amazed how in return your needs will be met and even surpassed. God gave Solomon more than He asked for, a fantastic payback for his sacrificial offering. Test God today by giving big to provoke a divine release of provisions in your favor.

The Prayer Solution

- Father, in your mercy, release your miracles to favor me in Jesus's name.
- Father, I plead that by your love, you will grant all my petitions in Jesus's name.
- Father, guide me to do all you require of me in Jesus's name.
- Father, bless me with resources to advance your kingdom in Jesus's name.
- Father, give me the grace to be a cheerful giver in Jesus's name.
- Father, remember me for good in Jesus's name.
- Father, may your countenance shine on me now and always in Jesus's name.

Receiving Your Covenant Blessings

Challenges

- When your big dreams do not manifest in the physical realm.
- When you face obstacles to your hopes and plans.
- When battles are too intense and frequent just before success comes.
- When too many failures precede and almost destroy your testimonies.

The Word Solution

Your possession is partly achievement and partly inheritance. Your possession is your God-given entitlement, your covenant right. One of your covenant rights is the divine assurance that no enemy will defeat you. You are to possess the gates of your enemies (Genesis 22:17); you will always take your enemies captive. Anyone attempting to take you captive will be taken captive (Revelation 13:10). Part of your divine entitlement is that weapons formed against you will always fail (Isaiah 54:17). God's intention is to bless believers and make them sources of blessing to the world (Genesis 22:18).

Being blessed means being successful. I hope you also know that being a blessing means becoming a channel through which God's favors will flow to others.

What do we see among believers today? It is a distressing fact that cannot hide. Too many believers are too poor. Instead of being vessels for healing others, they are in the grip of all manner of sicknesses and need healing. Instead of praying fruitfulness into the barren, they are suffering from barrenness. It is a travesty of the covenant blessings passed to us through Abraham, an inheritance confirmed by Jesus when He was made a curse so the covenant blessings would come to every believer (Galatians 3:13–14).

Many believers are missing out on their covenant blessings due to spiritual slothfulness. Covenant blessings cannot be taken up or retained effectively without a fight. That is why even after He had given the Israelites the Land of Promise, God still commanded them, "Begin to possess it and contend with (the occupying enemy) in battle" (Deuteronomy 2:24).

Many Christians just sit idly and complain or murmur. Lazy people cannot possess what is rightfully theirs. Joshua asked the seven tribes that had not yet received their inheritance, "How long are ye slack to go to possess the land, which the LORD God of your fathers had given you?" (Joshua 18:2–3).

You can fight for your covenant blessings only in holiness: "Upon Mount Zion shall be deliverance, and the house of Jacob shall possess their possessions" (Obadiah 1:17). Do not forget that this fight is spiritual and that your weapons are not carnal but mighty through God (1 Corinthians 10:4).

Get up and fight for your rights. The enemy is contending with you for most of the good things meant for you. You must fight to take them back. You are meant to be a blessing to the world. Nothing less is acceptable. I see you receiving your covenant blessings.

The Prayer Solution

- I possess my covenant blessings in Christ Jesus in His name.
- I command any diverted portion of my inheritance to be returned in full to me in Jesus's name.
- Every obstacle to my inheritance be removed in Jesus's name.
- Father, teach me and guide me to possess my possessions in Jesus's name.
- Father, strengthen me to fight for my inheritance in Jesus's name.
- Every foundational power against my inheritance be removed in Jesus's name.
- I recover my covenant blessings in the hands of my enemy in Jesus's name.

Divine Increase

Challenges

- When your lot in life is small and refuses to grow.
- When in business and family everything is stagnant and you desire a turnaround.

- When you are not achieving progress or increase.
- When you need heavenly help to advance and expand on all sides.

The Word Solution

In scriptural parlance, to increase is to flourish. Everyone desires increase. We all want our finances to grow. Parents wish for joyful enlargement of the family through childbirth. Pastors desire steady growth in their congregations' size and in church attendance just as principals want more students in their classrooms. Every businessman wishes for growth in terms of clients and sales, and doctors want more patients. A craving for increase is natural; it is a sign of prosperity, and it so often causes joy.

God promised the blessings of increase to man. He also expressly commanded man, "Be fruitful and multiply" (Genesis 1:28). Increase is a blessing from God and God alone. The first step toward genuine success is to partner with God. You must be a friend of God and be ready to sow and reap. Businesspeople sow their money to reap profit. Abraham was not pronounced the father of many nations until he was willing to sow his son, Isaac (Genesis 22:18). The remarkable thing is that God Himself gives seed to the sower. The seed He expects you to sow is in your hands already. Do not eat that seed; it is the capital for your sure increase.

Do you desire increase financially, spiritually, or in any other way? Are you already in increase and desire more? "The Lord shall increase you more and more; you and your children" (Psalm 115:14). God wants to increase you and your children, so partner with the Lord as Peter the fisherman did; he unconditionally released his boat to the Lord Jesus Christ for preaching, and Peter's reward was instant—his fishing business prospered dramatically (Luke 5:1–12). When Hannah released her boy, Samuel, to the service of the Lord, she received God's recompense of five more children (1 Samuel 2:20–21). Some years ago, a man of God asked me for a tie I was wearing, and gave it to him. Less than two weeks later, I got a gift pack of ten silk ties.

Only a partnership with God will guarantee you an increase. May God direct your ways on how to partner with Him that you may receive divine increase.

The Prayer Solution

- Father, grant me and my family increase in Jesus's name.
- Father, enlarge my coast spiritually and materially in Jesus's name.
- I overcome today whatever is obstructing my increase in Jesus's name.
- Father, command increase and prosperity to bless my endeavors in Jesus's name.
- Father, bless my every seed and make it yield a huge harvest in Jesus's name.
- Father, teach me how to partner with you for increase in Jesus's name.

Profitable Seed

Challenges

- When you want to learn how to sow to achieve a great harvest.
- When you wish to sow very profitably.
- When you doubt the benefit of sowing.
- When you feel wealth and prosperity are eluding you.

The Word Solution

Some farmers get carried away during harvest time and wind up consuming everything they harvest. But in every harvest is seed for the next harvest, seed that is meant for sowing then, not eating now. Every good farmer saves seed for the next planting season. The journey to a profitable harvest begins with a dutiful preservation of seed.

The next step toward a bounteous harvest is to clear and till the land and water it before sowing the preserved seed. A good farmer will tend his crops closely, weed his land regularly, and tackle the problem of pests, rogues, and other threats. He will pray for rain and clement weather, factors beyond human control that can make rich harvest.

Your seed is in the money or other resources you own. If you consume it all, you will have none to sow for a future harvest. If you set aside nothing, you may lack in the future. What you are enjoying today is the yield of yesterday's investment, its sown seed.

What you sow must relate to what you have (Mark 12:42–44) and what you are hoping to reap. If you sow little, you will reap little; if you sow big, you will reap big (2 Corinthians 9:6).

I once gave my old deep freeze to the wife of a minister in my parish. Within a month, I got a new job, and a send-off gift from my employers was a new deep freezer.

An important factor to consider is the kind of land you are sowing in. Is it a land that can fetch you a hundredfold return? (Mark 10:29–30). Only a land meeting the needs of God's kingdom is profitable for your sowing. And having sown, do you water your crops? You water your planting by prayer, evangelism, worship, and Bible study.

And what about weeding your land and guarding it against pests? That is warfare. You must fast and pray to remove what the enemy is planting among your crops. Whatever God did not plant must be uprooted (Matthew 15:13).

Get ready to fight powers against your seeds of profit. Kingdom profit requires commitment, and only the committed can take it by force (Matthew 11:12).

I see your harvest coming. You will dance with joy celebrating it.

The Prayer Solution

- Father, help me never to eat my seed as fruit in Jesus's name.
- Father, teach me to sow good seed correctly in Jesus's name.
- Father, show me good land worthy of my seed in Jesus's name.
- Father, as I water my plants with prayers, cause them to be fruitful in Jesus's name.
- Uproot any evil the enemy has sown among my crops, Father, in Jesus's name.
- I overcome all enemies of my divine investments, Father, in Jesus's name.
- Father, make all my sowing profitable in Jesus's name.

More than Enough

Challenges

- When you struggle with lack and insufficiency.
- When you crave a bounteous yield.
- When you desire abundant provision in the face of scarcity or lack.

The Word Solution

No man can ever meet all his own needs; he will always struggle for one thing or other. Even the rich have unmet needs and desires. As mortal men and women, we all are all limited in time and scope as well as in the ability to find, make, own, and apply or maintain resources. Not so our Creator, who is self-sufficient; the earth and everything in it belongs to Him (Psalm 24:1), and He still can command into being anything He needs.

God gives life and gives it abundantly (John 10:10). This attribute prompts Him to always give more than we ask of Him. It was a crisis situation when the multitude needed food and only two fish and five loaves were available, but God's answer to His Son's prayer turned that paltry ration into abundance. (Mark 6:43). God blesses you beyond your expectations and needs. If you are faithful in tithing, He will pour out for you a blessing you will not have room enough to store (Malachi 3:10).

God keeps His promises; He is waiting to prove Himself to you. Allow Him to be in your life because He is the God of more than enough in all situations. Reach out for a taste of His abundant blessings now and your cup will run over. His pipeline of overflowing blessings is open and running. Reach out in prayer, connect with Him, and receive His abundance. Our God will honor your seed with abundance if sown in faith and holiness; that is His way.

Recently, I sent three days' worth of cell phone credit to a minister of God, and about three days later, a protégé of mine sent me more than a month's worth of airtime, a tenfold return on the seed I had just sown. That is God for you.

The Prayer Solution

- Father, show yourself as the all-sufficient God in my life in Jesus's name.
- Father, show in every situation that you are more than enough in my life in Jesus's name.
- Father, beyond my expectation, supply all my needs in Jesus's name.
- Father, because I love you, give me what eyes have not seen and ears have not heard, what is beyond dream or imagination in Jesus's name.
- Father, let abundance become a way of life for me in Jesus's name.
- Father, because I honor you by giving my tithes to you, grant me your promised blessings so numerous that I cannot store them all in Jesus's name.
- Father, let your anointing on my head run over in Jesus's name.

Breakthrough by Diligence

Challenges

- When your labor is not enough and you need divine intervention to excel.

The Word Solution

Everybody wants to succeed, but many are not prepared to work hard for it. Some are simply lazy, and others are misguided; they wrongly believe they can achieve their breakthroughs by concentrating only on key spiritual exercises such as prayer and fasting without doing any work.

Friend, divine success does not work that way. Prayer is important and crucial, but success requires spiritual and physical effort in equal measure. God works even as Father and Son; Jesus made that point clear (John 5:17). We who are His disciples must also apply ourselves diligently to work. The world is established on the divine order of seed time and harvest time (Genesis 8:22), and no one should ever forget that.

There is due reward on this earth for diligence. The Bible affirms that a man diligent in his works will stand before kings (Proverbs 22:29). God will bless the work of our hands (Deuteronomy 28:12). But there are many in our midst today with no means of livelihood, but they expect wealth and riches. Which work of their hands are they expecting God to bless for them? One must be doing something no matter how small before God can add His blessings of harvest and increase.

Get to your duty post, good friend, and work—be productive. You cannot be watching movies at noon and imagine yourself on the way to success. Simon Peter worked "all the night" (Luke 5:5). He toiled while others were sleeping. God met him at his duty post in that encounter with Jesus and blessed the work of his hands mightily.

What are you doing that God can bless to make you wealthy? You must have a platform that showcases your diligence. An office? A shop? If you cannot get a paid job, create one. You can work from your home. What you need is not really salaried employment, and frustrating job searches sometimes get you nowhere. You need income from providing a service or product. Think about a need in your neighborhood that you can meet and be paid for providing. What you need is already inside you. What is your passion? What have you been configured to do? Get up and start doing it now. End any beggarly dependency on handouts, and let others start depending on you today.

My wife complains that I've worked too hard all my life, but I feel I have not worked hard enough. I believe I can do a whole lot more than I am doing; my productive capacity is far in excess of its results. I ought to keep driving myself to do better because there is still so much to do. I feel I haven't even started on the journey to success much less arrived there.

Diligence is the key to achieving the success we all dream about. Get up and get going—and keep at it. And don't just work—be sure to work hard for your success and God's glory.

The Prayer Solution

- Father, deliver me from the spirit of slothfulness in Jesus's name.
- Father, ignite the fire of hard work and diligence in me in Jesus's name.

- Father, help me engage and develop the work of my hands in Jesus's name.
- Father, encourage me to never give up in Jesus's name.
- I refuse to be lazy in Jesus's name.
- Father, connect me with diligent friends in Jesus's name.
- Father, reward my diligence with unlimited success in Jesus's name.

The Beginning of the Harvest

Challenges

- When you desire increase and great abundance.
- When you are frustrated with your humble circumstances and need a breakout.
- When you have sown much and need to reap the fruits of your labor.

The Word Solution

There is always a gestation period between seed time and harvest time. Good farmers are patient during the growing season. They know that seed time and harvest time will repeat endlessly (Genesis 8:22). They are people of great faith; they expect a harvest much greater than the seed they sowed. Those who sow on good soil expect the largest yield. Jesus referred to grades of good soil noting that some would yield a hundredfold, some sixtyfold, and some thirtyfold (Matthew 13:8). Farmers celebrate at harvest time; they live by the Bible truth that he who sows will doubtless rejoice at harvest time (Psalm 126:5–6).

Have you been engaging in intense prayers? Has your church been involved in intense praise and worship in the quest for open heavens? Have you been faithfully giving your tithes and firstfruits as offerings? All these amount to sowing. You have loaded your cloud, and the rain is about to fall for you. It's your harvest time, and God will show you that He reigns in the affairs of humanity. You will reap your fill. See the fields! The harvest is coming (John 4:35).

The Prayer Solution

- Father, the Lord of the harvest, command my harvest time to commence in Jesus's name.
- Release to me any portion of my harvest under contention by the enemy, Father, in Jesus's name.
- Father, dislodge every enemy blocking my harvest in Jesus's name.
- I destroy every spiritual pest or weed against my harvest in Jesus's name.
- Please give me seed to sow in your kingdom, Father, in Jesus's name.
- Fast-forward to me every delayed harvest in my spiritual farm in Jesus's name.
- Father, I am not planting for another to reap, so frustrate thieves eyeing my harvest in Jesus's name.

Chapter 6

Victory Capsules

Victory at Last

Challenges

- When your expected success is suddenly aborted.
- When your projects and programs fail despite your best efforts.
- When failure on the verge of success is a frequent occurrence.
- When you want to be the one to laugh last after a major battle.

The Word Solution

When the children of God enlist in the glorious army of Christ, they become targets of Satan and his evil forces. The devil's army on earth comprises forces the Bible refers to as powers, principalities, rulers of darkness of this world, and spiritual wickedness in high places (Ephesians 6:12). This evil army uses human agents in its wicked attacks against the soldiers of Christ.

Our Lord Jesus Christ is the Prince of Peace. His children find themselves drawn into mortal combat with the devil and his legions. Though neither aggressors nor warmongers, they must fight or be taken captive or be destroyed by the devil. The evil one is forever raging against them with his formidable arsenal of diseases, curses, arrows of failure, and even premature death. It is in line with his self-appointed ministry to steal, kill, and destroy (John 10:10).

Satan's attack on Jesus was meant to terminate Him as a person and as a divine being, but everything works together for good for those who love God (Romans 8:28). By His death, Jesus overcame death and hell for all humankind. He rose from the dead and ascended into heaven overcoming all principalities and powers and making an open show of them (Colossians 2:15). Jesus achieved victory. He laughed last and will keep laughing for eternity.

I once supervised a parish aptly named Victory at Last Parish. The worship center was a rented property in a posh, built-up area. It took sixteen years for the parishioners to find and buy a permanent place, but they were tenacious and did so; they bought a choice parcel of land there, and the church building is now complete.

In that church, a fifty-two-year-old woman of faith who had been barren for twenty-seven years gave birth to her first child. That congregation is witnessing scores of weddings these days. Victory at last—what a fitting name for your own coming testimony!

Jesus is our role model. Whatever we are passing through is not meant to overcome us. The scriptures are emphatic that we are more than conquerors (Romans 8:37). Even when it seems we are losing the battle of our finances, children, marriages, or even health, one thing is sure—we will win with Jesus at long last because He has overcome the world (John 16:33). We will win because He is greater than our evil foe (1 John 4:4).

In advance, I declare you the winner over all your troubles. Prepare to celebrate. Enthrone the Lord Jesus, and claim your victory in Him.

The Prayer Solution

- Father, help me to always realize that I am a soldier of Christ in Jesus's name.
- Father, equip me with spiritual weapons of warfare to enable me to fight and win the battles of life in Jesus's name.
- Father, you are my commander in chief. Never let me disobey you in Jesus's name.
- Father, may I never by any sinful act of commission or omission cause my demotion or dismissal from the army of Christ in Jesus's name.

- Father, as I fight the battles of life, never let me be discouraged and give up in Jesus's name.
- Father, strengthen me to go from victory to victory in Jesus's name.

Let God Rise

Challenges

- When you desire God to demonstrate His great powers in your favor.
- When enemies surround you and seem unstoppable.
- When you are yearning for God's urgent intervention in your matter.

The Word Solution

Kings sit on the throne and reign over their subjects. Heaven is the throne of God (Isaiah 66:1); He is the King of Kings whose footstool is the earth (Isaiah 66:1).

For a reigning king to rise from his throne to issue a command, the matter at hand must be crucial, extraordinary. A king rising to his feet to make an order bespeaks the full weight of the law being brought to bear on the matter at hand complete with the full majesty, glory, and power of the ruling house. This is what the Bible alludes to in the prayer "Let God arise and let His enemies be scattered" (Psalm 68:1). The moment God rises from His throne even without a word, all enemies and obstacles are decimated. When the Lord rises on your behalf, His glory is made manifest in you (Isaiah 60:2).

I pray that God will rise on your behalf. As He does, His enemies who oppose you will scatter and flee before Him (Psalm 68:1). His glory upon you shall be manifest, and any dark cloud covering His glory in your life will dissipate.

The King of Kings who reigns forever will rise on your behalf and take up your troubles as a job contract and fight for you so you can hold your peace (Exodus 14:14). I see you on the victory podium. Congratulations.

The Prayer Solution

- Father, I thank you for arising on my behalf in Jesus's name.
- God, rise on behalf of my family now and always in Jesus's name.
- Father, rise for all true believers who are suffering persecution everywhere in Jesus's name.
- Father, rise on behalf of the helpless, the destitute, the suffering, widows, orphans, and others in need Jesus's name.
- Father, rise on behalf of your church all around the world in Jesus's name.
- Father, rise on behalf of my country and guide us all into righteous living in Jesus's name.
- Father, in every emergency, please rise and fight for me in Jesus's name.

Overcoming Goliath

Challenges

- When you face major obstacles in your education, career, business, or other goals and objectives.
- When you feel intimidated or mocked by strong opposition.
- When your need for a great victory is desperate.

The Word Solution

For forty days, one man terrorized Israel (1 Samuel 17:16). He intimidated and mocked a whole nation, and nobody would confront him. When King Saul and the people of Israel heard his loud boastings, they were dismayed and were greatly afraid (1 Samuel 17:16).

Does this in any way resemble your situation? Is an enemy or problem so huge that it appears to be getting an upper hand over your life? Does a health problem of a loved one sound like a death verdict? Are you facing a financial challenge or a family crisis so severe that you and yours are gripped by terrible fear? Are you not in the same straits Saul and his subjects were in the shadow of the boastful giant Goliath?

Goliath had an intimidating presence; he seemed to be a physically insurmountable problem that could beset any believer. What is the Goliath in your life? Which of your problems has overawed you? What makes you think you cannot make history? Who is telling you that you will never do great exploits?

You must overcome your Goliath to make a difference as the young David did. It takes faith and courage. David dared while others ducked. Even when he stepped out to fight the giant, he received no real support. His superiors could only offer discouraging counsel; everyone including King Saul was afraid of the challenger's terrifying profile and exploits (1 Samuel 17:33). David had relied on God's help to slay a lion and a bear previously, and he faced the boastful Goliath in the name of the Lord God of Israel. The rest is history; David became a household name for heroism.

Some years ago, I had a boss who took a dislike to me for an unknown reason. He was a senior executive, and I, a lowly branch manager, found myself under the heavy weight of blatant oppression. I could fight back only with David's weaponry, the pebbles I threw at my persecutor through prayer. I regularly prayed with Psalm 35:1 asking God to fight for me against anyone who unjustly oppressed me.

On a visit to my branch one night, he slept in the guest house only to find in the morning that rats had eaten his shoes overnight. If God has to, He will send soldier rats to fight for you. Not long after that incident, he left the bank, and I was promoted to his position.

Your Goliath is in trouble. Just keep praying. If you want God to be glorified through you, confront and overcome your Goliath. Be not afraid of him. Take him on with absolute faith and trust in God, the owner of your life and his. It helps to recall as David did the battles God fought for you in the past. Jesus is the same yesterday, today, and forever (Hebrews 13:8). Like David, you must reject fear and discouraging counsel. Begin instead to see the reward for bringing Goliath to divine judgment. Fear not, for fear is not of God. You will prevail against your Goliath. I see you celebrating your victory in Christ.

The Prayer Solution

- Every source of reproach in my life be terminated now in Jesus's name.
- Father, thank you for the battles you helped me fight and win. Please accept my thanksgiving in Jesus's name.
- Father, in every battle of my life, be my enabler and strengthener in Jesus's name.
- I overcome every intimidating problem in my life by the blood of Jesus.
- I cut the head off every Goliath threatening my family in Jesus's name.
- Every stumbling block against my breakthrough be destroyed in Jesus's name.
- Every victory that should announce me to the world, Father, help me achieve in Jesus's name.

Paralyzing Satanic Agents

Challenges

- When agents of wickedness are dispatched against you.
- When you feel surrounded by servants of the devil.

The Word Solution

Satan has agents in witches, sorcerers, and occultists. Some of them might be dwelling under your roof. They may be blood relations or household help, but by spiritual links, they are demonic earth stations and satellites transmitting data to the devil. Satan's reliance on these agents is total and fundamental; unlike God, he is not omnipresent. He needs to spy, monitor, and eavesdrop continuously in his quest to steal, kill, and destroy. He must go to and fro gathering intelligence from his cohorts and seeking whom to devour. If his agents are incapacitated, he is rendered inoperative.

One of my favorite scriptures compares two warring houses, the house of Saul, which was waning weaker and weaker as the house of David was waxing stronger and stronger (2 Samuel 3:1).

There must be a drastic weakening of Satan's agents that are positioned against you. If not, you could be at great risk from their evil communications with their master. God can fight them for you, though, at your request if you are in good standing with Him. All your enemies will fall along with their helpers in the fight against you as God rises on your behalf (Isaiah 31:1–3). God may also choose to create enmity between them so they will fight one another (2 Chronicles 20:23).

Another interesting way God deals with Satan's agents is by rendering their weapons useless. He disappoints the devices of the crafty so that their hands cannot perform their enterprises (Job 5:12). That is why you took gunshots in your dreams but the bullets had no effect. That is why you drank poison asleep or awake and it caused you no harm. God decreed that no weapon formed against you would prosper (Isaiah 54:17).

Unless you can recognize Satan's agents, it will be extremely difficult if not impossible to fight and defeat them. You need help from God because only the Holy Spirit can expose these wicked spirits so full of guile and deception. As noted earlier, some may be dwelling under your roof. Some are office colleagues, and some operate even in churches. Satan can use anyone not filled with the Holy Spirit. You must therefore be very careful in choosing your friends and partners. Do not be unequally yoked with unbelievers (2 Corinthians 6:14–18). Be sober and vigilant (1 Peter 5:8), and test every spirit (1 John 4:1).

On identifying any agent of Satan, your spiritual duty is to neutralize him or her through effectual prayer. The enemy must never be ignored or allowed time or space for reinforcement. A serpent is best decapitated by the quickest physical means; so must a satanic agency be forcefully terminated by cutting off Satan, the head, from the possessed human body. This is a serious spiritual exercise involving prayer and fasting that will cast out the evil spirit and set the captive free.

As a disciple of Christ, you must pray, but avoid the common error of asking God to destroy all your human foes. Jesus commands that you bless those who curse you and pray for those who persecute you (Matthew 5:44). Leave any willfully wicked and unrepentant human agent of Satan to God, who knows how to deal with him or her. Scripture assures us that it is a righteous thing with God to recompense tribulation to them who trouble you (2 Thessalonians 1:6).

Assert your God-given spiritual and physical authority over your surroundings in a Christlike manner. There cannot be two captains of one ship. Rise and shine. I see you prevailing over satanic agents assigned to trouble you. Congratulations!

The Prayer Solution

- I command every agent of Satan assigned against me to depart from me and never come back in Jesus's name.
- I shut every door I opened to Satan or his agents consciously or consciously in Jesus's name.
- Father, expose every agent of Satan pretending to be a friend, relation, associate, or help to me in Jesus's name.
- Father, render useless all weapons Satan and his agents fashion against me in Jesus's name.
- Father, deliver me from every helper of my enemies in Jesus's name.
- I neutralize and displace every household informant of the devil in my life in Jesus's name.

Uprooting Evil Plants

Challenges

- When enemies plot evil against you.
- When colleagues conspire against you.
- When wicked people sow evil seed to bring you down.

The Word Solution

There are good plant and bad plants, and the bad can choke or crowd out the good. Weeds tend to grow faster than crops. The psalmist had that picture in mind when he sang so prophetically that the wicked might spring up like grass and flourish a while but that their end was destruction

(Psalm 92:7). Evil plants are sometimes mischievously introduced into a farm and planted by an enemy. Jesus told the story of the farmer who observing weeds or tares on his land lamented that only an enemy could have planted them (Matthew 13:28).

In many lives today, the devil and his agents are planting evil seeds, and sickness, death, and accidents are among them. Robbery, fraud, and theft are the devil's acts. Abortions, miscarriages, health challenges, and marital problems are the devil's tares, integral parts of his accursed works of stealing, killing, and destroying (John 10:10).

Thankfully, there is a solution. Jesus stated that every plant His Father did not plant must be rooted out (Matthew 15:13). The Word of God has the power to plant or root out, the power to establish or pull down. Jeremiah referred to this power when he declared that God had called on him to uproot and plant (Jeremiah 1:10).

You too can stand on the Word of God today. Do so and every planting of the enemy in your life would be uprooted be it in your home, business, church, or other relationships. Resolve your problems; quit tolerating sickness and destruction of your God-given assets. No farmer is happy with weeds or grass crowding out his crops. It is time you mobilize for weeding, time to recover your lost glory. Get into the mood of prayer. Now.

Some time ago, I came back from a prayer vigil with my wife, children, and our housemaid, who for some time had been behaving a bit weirdly. When we got to the gate of my house, she refused to enter the premises. She pointed at the roof in fright and alleged that a fire was burning there. My wife and I saw no fire, but no words could calm that girl down. She could not sleep that night, and she was gone the next day. What my wife and I could not figure out at that time was that God's love for us was at work on our behalf; He was making every evil eye, including our maid's, see the glorious fire of the Holy Spirit that was protecting my family. Witches and other demonic agents cannot be comfortable when God's awesome presence manifests as fire. It happened every night in the same manner for the children of Israel as they journeyed to the Promised Land (Exodus 13:21).

I pray that every weed God did not plant in your life be uprooted in Jesus's name. Raise the banner of victory in Christ. Command every disease to leave you and your loved ones calling each by name. Command the immediate cessation of miscarriages, marital crises, divorces and separations, child delinquency or delayed development, business setbacks, and any other affliction. Command all spiritual thieves to be exposed and arrested.

To the praise of God, I see those evil plants completely uprooted from your farm.

The Prayer Solution

- I command every weed God did not plant in me and mine to be uprooted in Jesus's name.
- Frustrate every enemy planting evil in my family, Father, in Jesus's name.
- Father, send men and women of goodwill my way so we can plant good seeds in one another's life in Jesus's name.
- I uproot every evil plant I inherited from my parents in Jesus's name.
- I uproot every weed choking the good plants in my life in Jesus's name.
- I command all sickness or disease in my body to depart in Jesus's name.
- I shut every door through which the devil plants evil in my life and command it to stay shut forever in Jesus's name.

Overcoming Foundational Limitations

Challenges

- If your parents and other ancestors were idol worshippers.
- If you have an idolatrous or demon-afflicted background.
- If you inherited an ungodly covenant.
- If there is a generational curse on your family.
- When there is a pattern of failure, ill health, or death in your family.

The Word Solution

If you build a ten-story house on a foundation meant for a five-story building, it will collapse. Jesus warned against building on a faulty foundation (Matthew 7:24–27). You need a strong foundation for your life as well if you want to grow.

Your foundation is your family roots. Do you know enough about your father and mother and their parents? How much do you know about your ancestors? Did any of them employ charms to secure their relationships? Did your father or mother consult evil powers before you were conceived? What shrine were you taken to at birth? What god were you dedicated to as a newborn? Is there any curse your parents inherited from your grandparents? Is there an unwanted common trait or evil pattern in your family? These are foundational issues that will define and shape your life to a large extent. They could limit your success in life as divine punishment falls on errant families up to the fourth generation for the sins of idolatry (Deuteronomy 5:9).

To the praise of God, there is a simple solution to this problem. You can destroy your bad foundation and build a new one today. Rejoice, friend, for it is a task you can do by the power of the living God. Our God has decreed by His uncommon grace that His children should no longer suffer for the sins of their ancestors (Jeremiah 31:29; Ezekiel 18:1–4). The qualifying criterion is to build on Jesus Christ, the Rock of Ages. No foundation should be laid except the one of Jesus (1 Corinthians 3:11). Jesus is the Word of God, the unshakeable foundation that outlives and outlasts everything in this world. Only a house built on the Word of God will stand the test of time. Only by the power of the Word of God can anyone resist the devil and the storms and troubles he causes. Weeping about your foundation will not remove its defects. Thank God for His Word that became flesh and redeemed us from every curse (Galatians 3:13–14). Every embargo on your success must be lifted. Pray against every foundational limitation.

One night some years ago, I dreamed I was running a race against two contestants. I was initially well ahead of them, but then I began to slow down. I stopped. I started walking backward. The other two runners passed me by. I found myself facing an idol in a shrine in my village. When I woke up, the Spirit of God ministered a Bible verse, Deuteronomy 5:9, that explained the dream to me. The point of it was that those behind me in life were overtaking me due to the burden of idolatry in my ancestry. I took immediate action by renouncing every covenant anyone in my lineage entered with that idol. To say that my life turned around not long after that is an understatement.

Friend, even if you have inherited curses or ungodly ancestral covenants or yokes, you are more than a conqueror when you appropriate the redeeming grace of God's Word in Ezekiel 18:1–4. Take control of your destiny, friend. I see your foundation rebuilt, and I will hear your testimony!

The Prayer Solution

- Father, rebuild whatever foundation I have built upon that is not of Jesus by your mercy and grace in Jesus's name.
- I renounce every evil foundation inherited from my ancestral line in Jesus's name.
- I break every evil covenant my parents entered on my behalf in Jesus's name.
- I break every curse flowing from my ancestral line in Jesus's name.
- Father, terminate every suffering emanating from the sins of my parents in Jesus's name.
- Father, the master builder of our lives and destinies, rebuild me today to fit your divine purpose in Jesus's name.
- I remove every foundational limitation in my life in Jesus's name.

Overcoming Evil Counsel

Challenges

- When people gang up on you.
- When malevolent counsel is put up against you.
- When even your benefactors are being turned against you.

- When others conspire to destroy or pull you down.
- When satanic networks and evil alliances form against you.

The Word Solution

Conspiracies are Satan's most common weapon he uses against God's children. Preceding or fueling it is evil counsel, and consequential to it is an evil attack. No child of God is immune to demonic gangs and plotters. They will surely gather but not by me the Lord said (Isaiah 54:15). Evil counsel aims at intimidating, trapping, and destroying the children of God to stop or mar His work.

The good news is that God assures His children that whoever gathers against them will fall (Isaiah 54:15). It is your heritage as a servant of the Lord that "no weapon that is formed against you shall prosper; and every tongue that shall rise against you in judgment you shall condemn" (Isaiah 54:17). God's express warning to evil counselors is that conspiracy against you, His child, will not stand and that anyone taking part in it will be broken in pieces (Isaiah 8:8–10).

The deciding factor is God being with you. He will frustrate the curses and plans of the wicked. Their gathering and counsel are in vain if God is with you. God's Word is emphatic—if He is with us, no one can be against us (Romans 8:31).

Friend, do you have the backing of God to face your trials with confidence? Only holiness and righteous living can guarantee you that confidence. God will not back adulterers, thieves, liars, cheats, fraudsters, pimps, murderers, or any other moral reprobate. Give back whatever you may have stolen, recompense those you have offended, and return to God in repentance. Only then can you "approach God's throne of Grace with boldness" (Hebrews 4:16) and take your place of honor as an anointed one of the Lord.

I see God laughing at anyone giving or taking evil counsel against you (Psalm 2:2).

The Prayer Solution

- Scatter all those conspiring against me, Father, in Jesus's name.
- I declare the counsel of every evil counselor hired against me of no effect in Jesus's name.
- May all those conspiring against me be broken in pieces in Jesus's name.
- Father, frustrate the plans of the wicked against me in Jesus's name.
- Father, deliver me from evil friends and companions in Jesus's name.
- Father, do not let the wicked succeed in any evil pursuit against me and my family in Jesus's name.

Achieving Total Victory

Challenges

- When your achievement is partial or incomplete.
- When you succeed in business but fail at home or vice versa.
- When you desire to sustain good success in every sphere of life.
- When your joy is mocked by reproach.
- When the enemy contends against your full triumph.

The Word Solution

I have heard of an outstanding corporate executive that is also a turnaround guru. He took a few failing corporations from the brink of collapse and turned them around with amazing success. A few years ago, he confessed that his success had come at the expense of his family. While he was succeeding in the corporate world, his wife divorced him and his family fell apart. He said his greatest regret was that he had no family to retire to after his much celebrated success in the corporate world. This happened because he had made no time for his family as he pursued success. A man who succeeds in business life but fails at home has incomplete success. Is your success absolute or incomplete? True success is absolute; God wants you to have it completely.

God's design for your life on earth is that you live holy and know, serve, and worship Him and prepare your soul for heaven. That is what Jesus meant when He said, "Seek ye first the kingdom of God and His righteousness and all (these) things shall be added unto you" (Matthew 6:33). God wants you to succeed and prosper in every aspect of life. He takes pleasure in your prosperity (Psalm 35:27). Jesus made Himself poor so that you can become rich. He wants you to enjoy good health (Exodus 15:26) and to prosper and be in good health as your soul prospers (3 John 2). That is total victory, absolute success.

A rich man who is always sick cannot enjoy his riches, and a healthy rich man who lives in sin and misses heaven is, simply put, a disaster. Do not succeed in church or business but fail at home. Do not succeed at home and business but fail in church. God wants you to succeed in every aspect of your life. Never ignore any aspect of your life—home, career, or church. Pray and work for it all, review your life, and take timely corrective measures. Fight on your knees for success in every facet of your life. It is a divine calling that none of us should fail to heed.

The Prayer Solution

- Father, strengthen me in every area of weakness in my life in Jesus's name.
- Father, help me run this race and finish well in Jesus's name.
- Father, help me pursue and achieve total success in Jesus's name.
- Father, deny me any regret at the end of my career in Jesus's name.
- Father, bless me with good health and prosper me in Jesus's name.
- Father, remove all obstacles to my total success in Jesus's name.
- Father, perfect everything concerning me in Jesus's name.

Breakthrough at Last

Challenges

- When you underachieve in spite of much effort.
- When you sense strong opposition to your breakthrough.
- When you want to overcome the enemy's resistance to your progress.

The Word Solution

Success involves winning battles. Enduring success involves defeating the enemy permanently. One of the greatest mistakes we make is thinking that achieving success is a piece of cake. Another common error is underestimating our opposition. Doing that has hurt me many times. The most naïve people believe they have no enemies. I have heard some friends say that nobody could hurt them since they had not hurt anybody; that is merely wishful thinking and self-deception. In the real world, the fact that you are holy and have never wished anyone evil makes you a big target for Satan, who opposes the righteous as certain as night follows day. Many are the afflictions of the righteous (Psalm 34:19), but God's deliverance is assured.

Our Lord and Savior stressed that a house divided could not stand. He was referring to Satan's forces and their sense of unity that holds them back from attacking each other. The enemy deliberately attacks you and everyone who does not belong to his kingdom. He fears what you will do for God's people if you become wealthy. He knows you would finance churches, fund evangelism, and sponsor missionaries—programs that depopulate his kingdom. He therefore raises storms of opposition against your finances to incapacitate and stop you.

In Genesis 26, Isaac's enemies blocked the wells he had dug. It was only after he had dug the third well that nobody strove again with him. He called the place Rehoboth: "The Lord has made room for us and we shall be fruitful in this land" (Genesis 26:20). Isaac achieved his breakthrough after two failed attempts.

Everyone faces some form of contention by the enemy. But just as

God rewarded Isaac for his trust and persistence, He will reward you, and you will enter your own Rehoboth no matter how many times you have previously tried and failed.

Welcome to your day of thanksgiving.

The Prayer Solution

- Father, reveal every strategy I need to employ to achieve an enduring breakthrough in Jesus's name.
- Increase every seed of breakthrough I have sown, Father, in Jesus's name.
- Father, equip and empower me to achieve beyond my dreams in Jesus's name.
- Father, spiritually, materially, and in every other way grant me breakthroughs in Jesus's name.
- I dislodge every power blocking my breakthrough in Jesus's name.
- Father, grant me the wisdom to work patiently for my breakthrough in Jesus's name.
- Convert every setback I have suffered, Father, to a morale booster to speed up my breakthrough in Jesus's name.

Overcoming the Real Enemy

Challenges

- When you need a way of escape from the enemy's onslaught.
- When you desire to silence the forces of wickedness.
- When you want to be an overcomer.

The Word Solution

My wife asked me an interesting question recently: "Why do men keep on falling for seductive women when all history is full of well-documented downfalls caused by such women?" My wife of twenty-eight years believes I have answers to all questions. I told her that the devil never introduces himself by name; otherwise, no sane man would fall for a temptress. The sex agent Satan has packaged and positioned to pull down servants of God would hardly ever turn up as a loose woman; she would more likely appear righteous, holy, and visibly committed to the service of God and maybe even speak in tongues. Only the Spirit of God can help a man discern a poisoned chalice.

We tend to forget how unbelievably patient and calculating the devil can be as he lies in wait for his prey. Delilah kept working on Samson until he became weary and lowered his guard. It is not for nothing that the scriptures enjoin us to watch and pray without ceasing.

Most women the devil uses to bring men down start out by showering men with gifts and kind gestures and eventually warm their way into their hearts. That in itself is not bad. The danger is when the recipient gets so carried away that he forgets himself. Any wonder why we must never cease praying for our pastors and spiritual leaders?

The devil who destroyed Samson is the same one who ruined Judas. The same evil one has brought down powerful politicians, top corporate executives, influential pastors, and some popular sports stars. The devil has not given up his evil ministry; he is an ageless spirit older than any human and therefore very experienced in using one thing or another to bring people down. He started his wicked craft in the days of Adam when he deceived Eve and through her Adam himself.

Considering the devil's long experience with messing up lives, no reasonable human being should ever mess with him. He brought down our ancestors. He knew everyone in our lineage, and he did all he could to tempt and destroy them. He knows our weaknesses and low moments; he sees where there is a chink in our armor. That is why he can use a teenage girl to bring down a great achiever, even a great servant of God.

Friend, be wise. The young beauty before you may be only eighteen, but the devil inside her is thousands of years old. But you can overcome the devil's wiles and onslaughts by being aware of your weaknesses be they pride, lust for money, inordinate craving for sex, or an unbridled desire for power and position. The devil is most likely to tempt you in your areas of greatest weakness.

Do not become overconfident. Most of those the devil brings down are so self-assured that they trust they could never fall. Such people pose a fascinating challenge to Satan, who goes to great lengths to bring them down. The Bible admonishes whoever thinks he is standing well to take heed lest he falls (1 Corinthians 10:12). We are to stay sober and vigilant because the enemy is a roaring lion moving around looking for whom to devour (1 Peter 5:8).

Only you can decide who owns your life and rules your body, soul, and spirit. Is it Christ or Satan? You become the servant of whomever you yield your will and obedience to (Romans 8:16). You can make your life an altar of the living God; the fire on it will never go out (Leviticus 6:13). No fly or pest survives a fire. Your body is the temple of the Holy Spirit (1 Corinthians 6:19). You must keep your fire burning through constant prayer, periodic fasting, quiet meditation, and regular fellowship with the brethren.

If you have fallen into the devil's trap by his temptations, realize that your moment of deliverance is here; whoever confesses and forsakes his sins will obtain mercy (Proverbs 28:13). Do not cover up or justify your sins but repent and confess them; God will then grant you forgiveness, cleanse you of all guilt, and restore you to righteousness as if you had never sinned.

I wrote this book for those who are facing temptation be it by a man or a woman, family, career, faith, or finances. As Joseph did, resolve to stay unsullied. Flee all wrongdoing. The grace of God is sufficient for you to overcome any temptation and not lose your destiny treasure. I trust my God that your testimony will soon be heard.

The Prayer Solution

- Expose every enemy in my life pretending to be a friend, Father, in Jesus's name.
- Father, give me grace to overcome the traps of the devil in Jesus's name.
- Help me overcome every weakness in my life, Father, in Jesus's name.
- Father, help me be sober and vigilant at all times in Jesus's name.
- Father, prevent me from taking any step that could make me fall into sin in Jesus's name.

- Father, help me keep the fire of the Holy Spirit burning in my life in Jesus's name.
- Father, deliver me from whatever trap I am in in Jesus's name.

Victory over Life's Battles

Challenges

- When you yearn for the keys of victory.
- When you are determined never to fail.
- When you are discouraged by previous defeats and need to recharge yourself.

The Word Solution

Life is full of battles. Someone jokingly said that newborns cry because they can see the battles they will face in life. Not even newborns are spared the fight for survival.

As children grow, they take on more and more responsibility for their survival. Every stage of life has its peculiar battles that we must fight by ourselves. If the battle for health is lost, death occurs. Losing the battle to get a good education results in trouble not just for an individual but also for all society. Adults engage in battles for employment, career progression, marriage, childbearing, parenting, and so on. Defeat in these battles results in pain, sorrow, and frustration. Without faith, we fall prey in our battles to frustration and temptation.

Life pits us in a fight against evils embodied in humans, communities, and institutions. We fight against spirits endlessly at home and everywhere else. Man born of woman is of few days and full of trouble (Psalm 14:1). Man is born to trouble (Job 5:7).

How then do we win this myriad of battles? The answer lies in a second question: who is backing you? Your backer determines whether you will win the battles of life. "If God be for us, who can be against us?" (Romans 8:31). God's backing is your only guarantee of success. No matter the storms of opposition, you are home and dry if God is with you. He promised to fight those who fight against you (Exodus 14:4).

He promised to confound your enemies and cause them to perish. He promised to hold you in His right hand of righteousness (Isaiah 41:10–13).

Many years ago, I worked in sales for a small company. It was alleged that I was among those bringing the company down. The boss had come under performance pressure from the board and was aiming to deflect the heat to his staff for the company's poor results, so I was promptly assigned impossible targets to achieve or be fired. The day before I was to be fired, there was a change in management and a new CEO emerged. The day that I was to be fired, I was actually promoted. God, who fought for me, will fight your battles for you too.

You cannot make it through life's battles without divine backing. Do not vainly assume that God is backing you; confirm and reconfirm your status in Christ by performing a spiritual checkup. If your spiritual scan does not show that you are free of spots, wrinkles, and blemishes, call on the God of Israel; He will help you in the day of trouble (Psalm 50:15). With God on your side, you will never lose any key battles in life.

The Prayer Solution

- Father, help me be sober and vigilant at all times in Jesus's name.
- Father, may I never let the fire on my altar go out in Jesus's name.
- Father, though I am a lawful captive of the devil by my sin and willful transgression of your Commandments, please deliver me in Jesus's name.
- Father, may I do nothing that gives room to the devil in Jesus's name.
- Father, may I not become my own enemy by neglecting your Word or disobeying you in Jesus's name.
- Father, ignite in me a hunger for your Word and strengthen me to pray in Jesus's name.

Power of Praises

Challenges

- When you imagine that prayer and fasting have failed you.
- When you yearn for God's presence but feel denied it.
- When you desperately desire entrance to the throne room of God.
- When you need God as the Lord of Hosts to fight for you.

The Word Solution

One can pray amiss, but one can never praise amiss. The only food God requires is praise. The twenty-four elders and the angels in heaven worship God day and night (Revelation 4:10–11).

To enter the court of God, you need to offer Him praise (Psalm 100:4). There is unlimited power in praising God. When Paul and Silas were locked up in prison, God intervened on their behalf when they offered Him praise (Acts 16:25). When the Israelites faced three allied forces, they cried out to God in prayer, but God basically directed them to organize a praise session instead to Him. They did so, and God intervened in the battle (2 Chronicles 20:17–24).

Nothing moves God as does the praises of His people. If you desire God's direct and manifest intervention in your matter, you must praise Him. God is ever faithful; He lives on the praises of His people (Psalm 22:3).

Have you ever spent a night just praising God? He is waiting for that kind of date with you. I see God intervening directly in your situation.

You may have heard a story Pastor Adeboye told many times of a newly wedded couple who went into the vestry with the officiating minister to sign the marriage register. The congregation was singing joyfully waiting for the newlyweds to be presented to the church. Unknown to them, the bridegroom had collapsed in the vestry and the unthinkable happened—he died. The smitten bride was in shock, and the congregation was left in suspense not knowing the sad news that awaited them. The pastors prayed all manner of prayers but to no avail, but someone remembered Pastor Adeboye's teaching on the effectiveness of praise even in the most dire circumstances. The moment the praying team began to praise God, the lifeless body sneezed, and in no time, the bemused bridegroom was back on his feet.

If prayer has not worked for you, please try praise.

The Prayer Solution

- Father, let your praise be continually in my mouth in Jesus's name.
- Father, give me hearty songs to praise you every day in Jesus's name.
- Father, dress me in a garment of praise in Jesus's name.
- Father, link me with your heavenly choir every time I want to praise you in Jesus's name.
- Father, every time I praise you, manifest your presence in Jesus's name.
- Father, as I praise you today, please intervene directly in every matter bothering me in Jesus's name.

Spend at least thirty minutes praising God now. Could you do it every day henceforth? Your life will be ever sweet as a result.

Winning with the Spirit

Challenges

- When physical efforts fail you.
- When human helpers let you down and friends or family cannot help.
- When you seek results beyond the ordinary to shock your mockers.

The Word Solution

When David offended God, his greatest concern was the possible separation of the Holy Spirit from him. He cried out to God, "Take not thy Holy Spirit from me" (Psalm 51:11). David knew he was dead without the Holy Spirit. He knew he would lose all the battles of life without the Holy Spirit's help. He knew he was down as a consequence of his sin against God, but worse still, he knew that if he lost the Holy Spirit, that would be his sorry end.

An obscure slave boy became the prime minister of Egypt due to a heathen king's observation that the Spirit of God was in the young lad (Genesis 41:38). That same Spirit, the Spirit of excellence, later distinguished another youth, Daniel, and his brothers in Babylon (Daniel 6:3).

We cannot win the battles of life without the Holy Spirit. We would be walking in the flesh, a sure prescription for disastrous failure. The lusts of the flesh will overcome the strongest defenses of carnal man. Only the Spirit of God can empower us to achieve victory; the Bible is emphatic on that point: "Walk in Spirit, and you will not satisfy the lust of the flesh" (Galatians 5:16).

Jesus did nothing in His life without the help of the Holy Spirit. Jesus's mother conceived Him by the power of the Holy Spirit (Luke 1:35). At His baptism in the Jordan River, the Holy Spirit rested on Him (Matthew 4:1). He grew in the Spirit (Luke 2:40). He was led by the Spirit of God into the wilderness to be tempted by the devil (Mark 1:12). Afterward, the Holy Spirit announced Him all over the region (Luke 4:14). He performed all His miracles by the Holy Spirit (Acts 10:38). He was resurrected by the Holy Spirit (Romans 8:11). He even asked His apostles not to preach until they received the Holy Spirit (Acts 1:8). If Jesus could not operate without the Holy Spirit and if He instructed us not to step out without Him, how could anyone succeed without the Holy Spirit? The battles of life are spiritual; we wrestle not against flesh and blood (Ephesians 6:12), and our weapons of warfare are not carnal.

Before I was baptized in the Holy Spirit, I considered studying the Bible as a herculean task. The Old Testament in particular was like a dull history book with those lengthy genealogies and boring passages. But after I was baptized in the Holy Spirit, divine illumination came to me in the Word of God; every verse I read opened my eyes, and they still do. Prayer and fasting, which used to be hard and punishing labor for me, have become not just easy but pleasurable.

No one should fight the many battles of life without securing the backing of the Holy Spirit. Whoever wants to learn the secrets of life must learn from the Holy Spirit, our heavenly teacher (John 14:26). Anyone in distress must turn to the Holy Spirit, our Comforter (John 16:7). Life is a battle we cannot win without the Holy Spirit.

If you want to become filled with the Holy Spirit, live a holy life because the Spirit is holy. If you seek the baptism of the Spirit (John 7:37), you will be filled to overflowing.

The Prayer Solution

- Father, forgive me for attempting to fight life's battles by myself in the flesh in Jesus's name.
- Father, baptize me afresh with the Holy Spirit in Jesus's name.
- Father, I have disappointed you many times, but do not take your Holy Spirit from me in Jesus's name.
- Father, distinguish me in all I do by your Holy Spirit in Jesus's name.
- Holy Spirit, empower me to fight the battles of life in Jesus's name.
- Father, allow me to grow daily as did Jesus in the Spirit in Jesus's name.
- Holy Spirit, become my senior partner in everything I do in Jesus's name.

Power of Decrees

Challenges

- When you seek God's intervention in your situation.
- When you desire a speedy resolution of your problems.
- When danger is so imminent that tomorrow seems too late.

The Word Solution

Decrees are absolute and irreversible orders issued by sovereign authorities; kings and monarchs issue decrees that must be obeyed by all their subjects. In general, decrees are not subject to negotiation or debate. In Ezra 1, King Cyrus issued a decree that Jews should be allowed to leave his kingdom and all his citizens should aid the departees with gifts of money. Everyone had to comply whatever their feelings about the matter were.

In the book of Esther, King Ahasuerus issued an offensive decree for the extermination of the Jews. The whole thing was instigated by the wicked courtier Haman. The endangered Jewish community had no option but pray for divine intervention.

Do you realize that you are a king? (Revelation 5:10). Do you know that you can by your decree issue a quit notice to sickness and other afflictions and they must obey? Do you know that you can issue a decree to poverty, barrenness, or chronic failure to flee you? In Christ, you have sovereign power over the devil and his agents, which the Bible calls serpents and scorpions. Our Lord Jesus has given you, His disciple, power over those forces (Luke 10:19). You will decree a thing and it will be so (Job 22:28).

The devil and his agents will never harken to your emotional pleas to leave your afflicted soul alone. Kingdom battles are not won by kid gloves but by the violence of faith actions. Cry no more over sickness or marital problems. Stop complaining about business failures. Rise and rule the issues in your life with faith-inspired decrees after having located God's promises in the scriptures concerning your troubling situations. Be sure to stand on those promises and issue all your decrees in the exalted name of Jesus. He is the King of Kings at the mention of whose name every knee should bow.

The Prayer Solution

- Father, help me realize and put to good use the great power you have invested in me in Jesus's name.
- I refuse to be under. From today on, I will be above in Jesus's name.
- I decree total deliverance for every member of my family in Jesus's name.

- I reject failure; I decree success in all my undertakings in Jesus's name.
- I reject defeat; I decree victory over every opposition to my destiny in Jesus's name.
- I reject sickness; I decree divine health in every part of my body in Jesus's name.

Fight for Your Inheritance

Challenges

- When your accomplishments in key areas of life are below those of your peers despite your best efforts.
- When you give up too easily.
- When you easily lose focus, drive, or interest.
- When you labor but others reap.

The Word Solution

We all expect to inherit something good from our parents—property, money, or other valuable assets. It may also be a social, political, or religious post or status. People can leave inheritances to their children (Proverbs 13:22), but their children have to take certain steps to gain their inheritance. One major first step is gaining the awareness that they have been left an inheritance and what exactly it is. Many have been robbed of inheritances because they had no detailed information on what was in their late parents' wills.

Do you know you have an inheritance in Abraham? "Abraham's Blessings are Mine" is a frequent song in church services. Are you one of the many who sing it without thought or basic understanding of its covenant rights and obligations? Some reflections on the scriptures including Genesis 22:16–18 and Galatians 3:7–14 would be quite helpful.

A second step in gaining your inheritance is to go for it; it will not come looking for you. That might entail a serious fight in some cases. When seven of the twelve tribes of Israel were yet to come into their possession (Joshua 18:3), Joshua charged them sternly, "How long are ye slack to go possess the land which the Lord God of your fathers had given you?" Joshua's words were a call on his countrymen to get up and fight for their territorial inheritance in Abraham.

Are you facing deprivation today? Get up and fight. Assert your authority and refuse to accept an inferior position. Insist on your right to prosper as a covenant child of Abraham. Insist on victory over your enemies. It is your right by inheritance.

A cousin of mine once went for a deliverance service and put in a good measure of prayer and fasting. In a vision of night, he saw a number of houses and motorcars. All were supposed to be his, but they were inexplicably locked up in a warehouse. He got the message and had to pray fervently for the warehouse doors to be opened so he could collect his entitlement. It was not long after that he acquired his first house. Today, he is inarguably one of my richest relations.

One thing though—whoever seeks the Abrahamic inheritance must do so with clean hands and in holiness. A sinner cannot inherit Abraham's blessing. The Bible is unequivocal on that point: "Upon Mount Zion there shall be holiness and the children of Israel shall possess their possessions" (Obadiah 1:17).

Go today for your inheritance of covenant blessings. It is your testimony in waiting.

The Prayer Solution

- I possess my inheritance in Abraham now in Jesus's name.
- Father, open my eyes to see my inheritance as a child of Abraham and your child in Jesus's name.
- Loose your grip any force contending against my inheritance and be turned back in Jesus's name.
- Blot out any sin in my life that is stopping me from possessing my possessions, Father, in Jesus's name.
- Every door shut against my inheritance, open and release it in Jesus's name.

Chapter 7

Capsules for Open Doors

The Power of Prayers

Challenges

- When in need but not knowing how to meet the need.
- When you want God's quick intervention and solution to your problems.
- When you are tired of murmuring and complaining.
- When your challenge is beyond human agencies and professionals (doctors, lawyers, bankers, etc.).

The Word Solution

Prayer is an appeal, a request to someone with authority to grant you a favor. Prayer is a plea for intervention, and praying to God is a privilege of believers who understand God does not intervene in human affairs except and until they pray. Jesus taught us how to pray (Luke 11:1–13), and He prayed regularly; hence, the biblical injunction that we should pray without ceasing (1 Thessalonians 5:17).

The challenge most people face is their predisposition to complain instead of pray. Most people murmur rather than petition the almighty God in prayer. The children of Israel were like that in the wilderness—murmuring ceaselessly instead of talking to their God in prayer. God was so upset with them that He allowed them to face fiery serpents for a season (Numbers 21:5–6).

What challenges are facing you today? How many of them have you tabled before God in prayer? Even if the answer has yet to come, have you kept knocking on heaven's gate, or have you tamely surrendered to defeat? Jesus says we must persist in prayer until God answers. As true believers, we must seek till we find, ask till we receive, and knock till the door is opened (Matthew 7:7). That kind of persistence may sometimes entail waking up at midnight to pray. Jesus prayed all night in the Garden of Gethsemane, the sweat pouring out of His body like thick drops of blood.

When you are faced with difficult problems, rouse yourself to pray at night. Sometimes, it is necessary to add a stretch of fasting to the praying. One way or another, stop fruitless lament and unhelpful complaining about your problems. Stop broadcasting your misfortunes to others because they have their own issues. Take your problems to Jesus in prayer. He is waiting to set you free.

The Prayer Solution

- Father, I repent of all my past murmurings and complaints. Please show me mercy and forgive my lack of faith in Jesus's name.
- Father, I resolve from today to never again shed tears before anyone; I will cry out only to you in Jesus's name.
- Father, in your mercy, teach me how to pray in Jesus's name.
- Father, as I pray to you, open the heavens and shower me with your blessings in Jesus's name.
- Prevent whatever can cause unanswered prayers, Father, in Jesus's name.
- Father, give me the grace of tireless and unrelenting prayer in Jesus's name.
- Father, see me through testimony of answered prayers in Jesus's name.

Open Doors

Challenges

- When setbacks and disappointments are more the rule than the exception.
- When you suffer rejection and undeserved hurt.
- When you are denied whatever you are fairly due.
- When you are not given a fair chance to present your case.
- When an opportunity that is open to all closes when it is your turn.

The Word Solution

Valuables are normally kept behind closed doors secure from theft and other hazards. The level of security and access depends on their value. Jesus described Himself as the door (John 10:9) and the only way to the Father. This means that nobody on earth can have access to the riches of God unless Jesus grants that access.

There is a door for everything in creation. Heaven itself has doors (Psalm 78:23), the seas have doors (Job 38:8), and even death has a door (Job 38:17). Jesus Christ was revealed to humankind as the one and only holder of the key of David that can open and shut any door (Revelation 3:7–8). Only He can open the doors of blessings and favor, and only He can shut the doors of death and failure for whomsoever He wills.

A door of grace may be open in the spirit realm, yet human entrance thereto may be hindered by Satan. The apostle Paul experienced such a lamentable situation. He wrote that even though a great and effectual door was opened to him, there were many adversaries (1 Corinthians 16:9). The good news for the children of God is that Jesus is the Lord of Hosts and the head of all principalities and powers. Call on Him today. He will rise on your behalf and scatter every contention against the doors He opens for you.

Whatever your challenge, call on His name and every door you want opened will be opened. Prayer is tantamount to knocking on the door. Knock and it will be opened for you (Matthew 7:7). The Holy Spirit opened the door of Jesus's tomb with an earthquake. The same Spirit will open every closed door of blessing in your life.

The Prayer Solution

- Father, open every beneficial door the enemy has shut against me in Jesus's name.
- Father, close every evil door the wicked has opened to attack me and my family in Jesus's name.
- Father, give me the master key to the door of total victory in Jesus's name.
- Father, open the heavens over me from today on in Jesus's name.
- Lord Jesus, you are the door. Grant me access to heavenly riches, and may your name be glorified, amen.
- I command every satanic agency blocking my open doors to be arrested and detained now in Jesus's name.

Breaking Conspiracy

Challenges

- When colleagues and relatives form evil alliances against you.
- When household enemies manifest against you.

The Word Solution

The greatest mistake you can make is to think everybody loves you. The truth is that the more successful you become, the more your known and unknown haters increase. In the same vein, the closer you get to God, the more your spiritual enemies will increase. One tactic the enemy uses to fight believers is conspiracy, the coming together of satanic forces to fight children of God. The wicked conspire to strike, the best time and place to do so, and the most lethal weapons to deploy.

The good news for every child of God is that God knows this and every other tactic of the devil and has readied appropriate defenses for them. God emphatically forewarns that the wicked will conspire against you, His dearly beloved. He, however, makes it quite clear to the enemy that they have neither His mandate nor His approval to do so and that their evil alliance will fall for your sake (Isaiah 54:15). He does not stop evil ones from conspiring against you, but whatever they do, their counsel will not stand and they will be broken to pieces (Isaiah 8:8–10).

Lose no sleep over the enemy's conspiracies because those engaging in it are wasting their time and energy. All their plans against you will come to naught as you simply call on God. Their armies will be scattered. They may have come one way, but they will flee seven ways. Then you will peaceably enter the door of testimony the Lord God has opened for you.

The Prayer Solution

- Every satanic alliance against me be scattered now in Jesus's name.
- All witchcraft networks against my life be shattered in Jesus's name.
- Every satanic conspiracy against my soul be terminated in Jesus's name.
- Father, may the evil forces fighting me be turned against one another and may they never prosper in Jesus's name.
- Father, destroy every evil altar aiding or abetting the fight against my soul in Jesus's name.
- Father, rise and condemn to utter failure any malicious gang orchestrated against my service to you and to all humanity in Jesus's name.

Open Heavens

Challenges

- When blessings just do not come your way.
- When your prayers remain unanswered.
- When you feel frustrated and stressed and wonder if you are under a curse.

The Word Solution

God is in heaven, and earth is His footstool (Isaiah 66:1). His presence is everywhere and in everything, but He has a throne and a palace.

No king rules without a palace. God is the King of Kings who rules from heaven over all His creation. If He decides to shut heaven, there would be no rain on earth (Revelation 11:6). He may choose to shut either the windows or the doors, or He may do a complete shutdown.

God's hand is moved to open the heavens by worshipful acts of His faithful servants on this earth. King Solomon moved heaven and its visible glory by rendering stupendous offerings and astounding praise to God (2 Chronicles 5:7–14). As a believer, you too can do the same by faithful tithing; your acceptable sacrifices open heaven for a downpour of divine blessing (Malachi 3:10).

The heavens opened for Jesus when he was baptized (Matthew 3:16). The obvious implication is that heaven is selective regarding whom it opens to. It can be opened to one person and shut to another standing next to him.

The secret of answered prayer is open heavens. Enter the gates of the Lord with thanksgiving and into His court with praise (Psalms 100:4, 95:2). In God's presence is fullness of joy and pleasures forevermore (Psalm 16:11). That's another name for open heavens.

Are you burdened with loads of unanswered prayers? It is possible that your heavens are shut? Have you considered losing yourself in good old corporate worship? Go praise God for seven straight days and thank Him for all He has done for you to date. You have asked enough. God is not deaf. Change your approach. Render praises. Move God to open the heavens. Praise Him. Do it with the same level of energy with which you pray. Instead of vigil nights of prayers, engage in vigil nights of praise and worship.

I see you testifying of answered prayers. Welcome to open heavens.

The Prayer Solution

- Father, if my sins caused your heavens to be shut against me, I ask by your mercy and grace that you please forgive me in Jesus's name.
- You evil clouds blocking my heavens be blown away by the wind of God in Jesus's name.
- Father, please open the heavens over me and my family and grant us your fullness of joy and pleasures forevermore in Jesus's name.
- Father, may I never again labor under closed heavens in Jesus's name.

Get Up and Fight

Challenges

- When you feel defeated and embittered.
- When you have endured long oppression.
- When you feel stale in one location and wish to move elsewhere.

The Word Solution

Believers are taught to be very tolerant and patient. Long-suffering is taught as a great virtue, and every Christian is encouraged to learn to wait on the Lord. There are scripturally promised rewards for patience in waiting for God's appointed time. Those who wait on the Lord will renew their strength (Isaiah 40:31). Generally, God's promises necessitate waiting, which at times is God's way of testing believers' faith. Waiting on God and His promise is therefore a sound biblical doctrine not to be downplayed.

But the Bible never told us to wait on the devil. The Bible never taught us to exercise long-suffering in favor of demons who are attacking us. We are not to ever be patient with the devil or his agents, and we must not confuse waiting on the devil with waiting on God.

Many things you ask of God are promptly released from heaven, but Satan and his agents block them from getting to you. That is what happened to Daniel, who had to wait twenty-one days to receive the goods God had speedily dispatched to him on the day he commenced his prayer for them (Daniel 10:12–13). The devil was blocking them, and it took a serious spiritual battle to defeat him. How much quicker would have been the delivery if Daniel had prayed with knowledge.

The spiritual enemy of humankind is very stubborn. He hinders and tries to confiscate your blessing and will never release it without a tough battle. Stop worrying God for the miracle He has already mailed you, and start fighting the devil to release what he has stolen or blocked.

God gave you power over the devil (Luke 10:19); rise and use that power today. Don't be nice and gentle with a burglar you have caught red-handed. David pursued and overtook the Amalekites and recovered all they had taken from him (1 Samuel 30:1–18). If the chariots of Pharaoh are chasing you, the Red Sea will show them no mercy (Exodus).

I am tired of fainthearted believers. I get angry at Christians who beg Satan to leave them alone. I am tired of hearing believers tell stories of their severe buffeting by the devil and believe that is their cross. I get angry at believers who forever worry God with issues that God has fully empowered them to handle by and for themselves. I want to see strong and active believers (Daniel 11:32), Christians living in dominion (Genesis 1:26), and the devil under their feet (Romans 16:20).

You have to enlist in that number. Get up and fight. Tonight, organize a family vigil. Decree a new lease on life for yourself and your family in the mighty name of Jesus. Stand by that decree and it will come to pass. Nothing really moves until someone moves it. Be the mover. Make things happen. Challenge the real enemy. Fight for your miracle. The time is now.

The Prayer Solution

- Every long outstanding problem in my life be resolved now in Jesus's name.
- Any pharaoh seeking to manipulate my destiny loose your grip or drown in the Red Sea in Jesus's name.
- Every altar speaking evil into my family be destroyed in Jesus's name.
- Expose and disgrace every satanic priest aiding or abetting crises against me, Father, in Jesus's name.

- Father, as Pharaoh and his army drowned in their vain pursuit of your children, so be it for any power chasing me or working to hinder my progress in Jesus's name.
- Father, deliver me from the captivity of wicked spirits in Jesus's name.
- Every enemy grappling with my blessings and miracles loose your hold now in Jesus's name.

New Open Doors

Challenges

- When you want new career or business opportunity.
- When you want a new lease on life.
- When your present situation feels like a dead end.
- When you must make a life-changing move.

The Word Solution

A new door in this context is one that did not exist previously, a fresh opportunity to access a need or desire. It may also be a chance for a status change that was not there before. Think of Joseph in Pharaoh's Egypt (Genesis 41:41). Before and after him, there was no office of prime minister in that land; that position was created for him. That was a new door divinely created for one man who was languishing in prison before the glorious day he stood before Pharaoh.

God will always do new things. He will make a way in the wilderness. (Isaiah 43:18–19). There are neither sure roads nor clear footpaths in the wilderness, but God will make one for you in your hour of need, a path of safety in time of crisis and confusion. He always opens new doors for His trusting children so they can keep marching to their destiny.

You will march through a new door that is meant for you alone. Trust in God to see you through that wilderness. You may be suffering wrongful imprisonment at the moment, but your God is not unaware of the situation. He still has your destiny in His charts, and He will fashion the needful new door that is certain to get you there.

The Prayer Solution

- All doors bringing pain and sorrow into my life be shut in Jesus's name.
- Father, open for me and my family a new door of blessings in Jesus's name.
- Father, open a door for me that has never opened for anyone else in Jesus's name.
- Father, open a door for me to take your gospel to the world in Jesus's name.
- Father, open a new door of prophecy for me in Jesus's name.
- Father, remove every adversary to my open doors in Jesus's name.

Divine Instruction

Challenges

- When you need a miracle but wonder what God wants you to do to get it.
- When you wonder why God favors some people with explicit commands.
- When you wonder why some divine instructions seem ridiculous.

The Word Solution

Most often, God's miracle for someone is preceded by His instruction meant to profit the individual to whom He gives it. To make Abraham a great man, God ordered him to move to a land He would show him. Abraham obeyed. The rest is history.

Isaac followed his father's example of obeying the divine will when he obeyed God's instruction not to leave Gerar, a place that did not favor him at first. The result of his obedience was a divine reward—God prospered him in that country. He attained wealth that made him the envy and dread of all (Genesis 26:1–15). At the wedding in Cana, Jesus told the stewards to fill pots with water and serve the contents. As ridiculous as that seemed to the stewards, the best wine flowed from the pots. In Luke 17:11–19, Jesus healed ten lepers only by asking them to go show themselves to the priest. They did and were cleansed.

Your problem is unresolved because you have yet to receive a divine solution to it. Listen to and obey God's instructions that will solve that problem. It is possible that God had spoken to you already. You might have forgotten that, or perhaps you did not even take notice or never heard Him at all. Ask Him again. He will answer you and show a depth of revelation that you could not have imagined (Jeremiah 33:3).

Some time ago, God instructed me in a vision to apply to a certain big bank for a job. I applied as directed, but a different and much smaller bank responded to my letter and called me in for an interview. I had absolutely no idea that the banks were related. I got a job in the small bank, and five years later, it was acquired by the one I had initially applied to. God knows tomorrow. He knew there was no vacancy in the big bank at the time, but He made me apply for a job there because He knew that the acquisition would happen in five years; He prepared for me a place there.

The moment you hear God's instruction, obey it. Doing so will earn you a fabulous miracle. Ask for grace to obey God's word of instruction.

Your miracle is knocking on your door.

The Prayer Solution

- Father, help me hear and recognize your divine instructions in Jesus's name.
- Father, give me the grace to obey your directives without delay in Jesus's name.
- Father, let me know what I need to do to be whom you made me to be in Jesus's name.
- Help me stop doing whatever is contrary to your instructions, Father, in Jesus's name.
- Father, may I never dismiss or disregard any instruction from you or treat it as ridiculous in Jesus's name.
- Father, remind me please of whatever word you gave me that I have forgotten in Jesus's name.

Open the Prison Doors

Challenges

- When in a dream you see yourself under arrest or in detention.
- When you see yourself in a dream being tried in a court.
- When you find yourself moving in circles.
- When your life's pattern consists of rises and falls.

The Word Solution

This may shock you, but many people you see every day are prisoners. Several are actually in handcuffs and leg chains. The only reason their prison cells and iron fetters are not visible to the naked eye is that their imprisonment was ordered and effected beyond the physical realm. It is an act of wickedness executed in the realm of the supernatural. Unknown to many, it is the spirit realm that controls the physical realm.

To bring this revelation closer home to you, have you ever seen yourself in a dream being arrested by policemen? Have you ever dreamed of appearing before a judge without a lawyer at your side and hearing charges read against you? Have you ever dreamed of being locked up in a room with no way of escape?

Many would dismiss such dreams with a wave of the hand, but they have not read the Bible or do not appreciate the grace of God that speaks to His people through dreams in these last days (Joel 2:28). It is unfortunate that not everyone God is speaking to is hearing or listening to Him. It is also tragic that not all who hear are able to understand Him or are willing to obey Him.

You may be one of those who are moving around in circles by reason of spiritual imprisonment. You are making no progress in life because the high walls of your spiritual prison permit neither progress nor freedom. You are caged, unable to free yourself. But your situation is not as hopeless as you think. You can choose how to respond to the challenge. Will you remain comfortable with your lot as a prisoner, or will you wish to break loose this minute? Will you lie down and do nothing, or will you act like Paul and Silas, who rose to their challenge? (Acts 16:25). The two men prayed and sang praises to God, and He released them from prison. Freedom from prison physical or spiritual is God's will for all. Jesus came to this world to set the captives free (Luke 4:18; Isaiah 61:1).

Under imprisonment, can you prosper or even do any profitable business? If you are in handcuffs, how can you receive anything? Your physical condition is only a manifestation of the settled order in the realm of the Spirit.

You cannot achieve your destiny if you remain in prison. You cannot secure the job of your choice or pursue a worthwhile career while being a prisoner. Joseph the dreamer was helpless in prison, but out of prison, he was a transformed figure. He became prime minister, got married, fathered children, and brought his father and family to Egypt. He even executed a plan that helped the whole world survive a dreadful seven-year famine.

Cry out to God now! Praise Him in the worthy example of Paul and Silas. I see your chains and handcuffs breaking loose. I see your prison doors opening. I see you stepping out of prison and fulfilling your destiny. Praise the Lord some more.

The Prayer Solution

- Every satanic judgment against me be annulled now in Jesus's name.
- Every evil accusation levied against me be set aside now in Jesus's name.
- Any spiritual power holding me in prison release me now in Jesus's name.
- Every satanic chain or handcuff holding me bound be broken now in Jesus's name.
- Every evil in my life be reversed now in Jesus's name.
- Father, grant me grace to understand and interpret dreams correctly in Jesus's name.
- Father, release me and my family from spiritual prison in Jesus's name.

Overcoming Sin

Challenges

- When you live a life of sin you sincerely wish to stop.
- When you keep failing in efforts to live a holy life.
- When sin is a bondage you feel incapable of escaping.
- When you keep going back to a habitual sin and don't know why.

The Word Solution

Sin is disobedience to the Word of God. The devil has no power over true Christians. The only real enemy is sin. It opens the door and empowers the devil to come in and do as he pleases. Sin causes Christians to lose the divine grace that protects them from Satan's weapons. Sin causes God to turn His face away from them. It brings destruction or terrible afflictions to them. David recognized that he was afflicted because he had gone astray (Psalm 119:67).

Sin could cost you all the good things of life. It attracts curses even from God (Deuteronomy 28:15–68). A major challenge is keeping sin out of your life. Some have allowed sin to become their master. But companionship with Jesus makes it impossible for us to sin. Power over sin is available to us only when we eat, drink, and live in Jesus. He was wounded for our transgression (Isaiah 53:5). He purchased our sin by taking a severe beating for it. He took it over. He took our place on the gallows. He died for our sins.

Jesus is the Light and the Truth. Sin is a lie from Satan, the father of lies and the prince of darkness. If you have Jesus, you have the truth and the indwelling light of God so you will not sin, which leads to death (Romans 6:23). Jesus is life (John 14:6). If you have the life of God, you cannot sin. He is the way (John 14:6), and anyone living in sin has missed the way. Walk with Jesus and you will not miss the way. Sin is in the world, but Jesus in you is greater than the power of sin (1 John 4:4).

Your question may be how Jesus could dwell in you. The answer is up to you because Jesus is the Word of God who became flesh (John 1:1–14).

That same Word is spirit and life (John 6:63), and it is written in the Bible for you to read, memorize, meditate on, internalize, and live by.

Get going today. Read the Bible and enrich your mind with the Word of God. Fill yourself with it and the Spirit of Jesus will come alive in you. Be baptized by the Spirit of God and you will learn to live in the Spirit and hear and obey God's instructions. You will begin to walk in the Spirit and overcome the lusts of the flesh (Galatians 5:16–21). God's Spirit will dwell in you and give you His power to control your thoughts, words, and actions.

Seek the full baptism of the Holy Spirit. You will dump the worthless life of flesh, step up to the fulfilling life in the Spirit, overcome sin, and become a vessel of blessings. God will confirm all words you speak on His behalf with signs and wonders. You will decree things in righteousness and they will come to pass.

The Prayer Solution

- Father, give me special grace to live holy every day in Jesus's name.
- Father, deliver me from any form of bondage to sin in Jesus's name.
- Father, hide me in your secret place in Jesus's name.
- Father, help me discern every trap or temptation in Jesus's name.
- Father, strengthen me to overcome temptations in Jesus's name.
- Father, you are the true light. Shine on me always in Jesus's name.
- Father, you are life and spirit; live in me and enable me to control my thoughts, words, and actions in Jesus's name.

Secrets of Answered Prayers

Challenges

- When you desperately need answers to your prayers.
- When you are troubled with unanswered prayers.

The Word Solution

Some prayers yield no answers. Some are said amiss, and some come from wrong motives or impure hearts. Many people pray routinely but scarcely care to find out why their prayers are not answered. Certain facts about praying to God cannot be ignored. God is Spirit, and those who worship Him and pray to Him must do so in spirit. God does not hear sinners (John 9:31). In God's eyes, the sacrifices of the wicked are an abomination (Proverbs 21:27). If you are not on good terms with God, what right do you have to expect or demand that He help you? Why do you expect Him to answer your prayers when you are not in right standing with Him? God made it clear that He would not hear your prayers if you disobey Him (Isaiah 59:2). How then do you expect Him to answer what He never heard? He warned that if you do not answer when He calls you, He will laugh when you are in trouble (Proverbs 1:26).

First, reconcile with God by genuine repentance and confession of sin. Otherwise, your prayers are a waste of time and effort. They cannot go beyond the roof.

Most of us often bombard heaven with our prayers before we confess our sins. We might be prayer warriors who are nursing grudges against others. One person might commit adultery the day before he prays, and another might commit fraud at work but expect his prayers to be answered.

God has His principles. He is sovereign. He made the rules, and we must follow them as it is simply not possible to deceive Him. God will not be mocked (Galatians. 6:7).

We read in the Old Testament that the priest could not enter the holy of holies unless he had offered an acceptable sacrifice to cleanse himself with the blood of a lamb (Hebrews 9:6–9). Cleansing was necessary to obtain mercy. That principle has not changed. The only difference in the New Testament is the Lamb of God, whose blameless and spotless blood was shed once and for all time for the atonement of sins. The Son of God offered Himself on the cross of redemption for all humankind. By His shed blood, we can now boldly enter the holy of holies having obtained mercy by the washing away of and forsaking our confessed sins (Proverbs 28:13).

You may need to reset your prayer pattern. First, make peace with God before you begin to sweat out your prayer requests. Ask for mercy first, and confess your sins and your unworthiness. Be humble in spirit, and God will show you mercy and open doors in answer to your prayers.

May God show you the depths of His mercy today and always.

The Prayer Solution

- Father, my sin is weighing against me; please show me your mercy and forgive my sin in Jesus's name.
- Father, by the blood of Jesus, wash away my transgressions and blot out the record of sin that is against me in Jesus's name.
- Father, when I pray amiss, please set it aside and set me right in Jesus's name.
- Every prayer I pray according to your will, Father, please answer in Jesus's name.
- Father, help me pray in holiness at all times in Jesus's name.
- Father, show me mercy every day in Jesus's name.
- Father, guide my thoughts and prayers in Jesus's name.

Power in God's Mercy

Challenges

- When you need God's total forgiveness.
- When you want God to promote and bless you.
- When you want God's favor in spite of your failings.
- When you need divine attention.

The Word Solution

One of God's eternal principles is the punishment He reserves for sin. Adam and Eve got theirs in the Garden of Eden when they disobeyed His one and only command. God made it clear to Moses that the Israelites had to choose between obeying His laws and receiving His blessings or breaking them and reaping His curses (Deuteronomy 30:19).

Whenever the Israelites disobeyed God by worshipping idols, they were punished. In extreme cases, God went as far as handing them over to their mortal enemies. God is just and righteous; hence, the punishment He gives for any offense is appropriate. Sometimes, because of His infinite mercy, the punishment is smaller than deserved, but such divine grace does not void His utter displeasure with sin. The wages of sin is death (Romans 6:23). David was a man after God's heart, but not even he could completely escape God's judgment for his sins.

Some have wondered why sin today doesn't appear to be punished instantly. The answer is simple—God's mercy. God delights in showing mercy (Micah 7:21), and it is because of God's mercy that we are not consumed (Lamentation 3:22). The crucifixion of our Lord Jesus Christ was a defining moment for the atonement of sin for all humankind. It ushered in the ultimate grace of God as it was the perfect sacrifice. In the succinct words of the Bible, mercy came through Jesus (John 1:11). The blood of Jesus avails mercy. When we plead for forgiveness of our sins, the blood of Jesus speaks mercy on our behalf before the throne of God; it is the restraining factor when God's wrath for our sin is provoked. If we confess and forsake our sin, we will obtain mercy (Proverbs 28:13).

But divine mercy must never be taken for granted (Romans 6:1) or abused. God is a loving Father who wants you, His straying child, to come home. He needs you to forsake your sinful ways and plead for the mercy He freely offers. Take advantage of it as His rightful child, be wise, and reconcile yourself with Him, your Father. Welcome to the extraordinary mercy of God.

The Prayer Solution

- Father, show me your mercy everywhere I go in Jesus's name.
- Father, never let your mercies run out on me in Jesus's name.
- Father, show me the mercy you showed David in Jesus's name.
- Father, in your mercy heal me of every sickness or defect in Jesus's name.
- Father, add me to the ranks of your chosen and highly favored, those you show mercy to always in Jesus's name.

- Father, may I never lose your mercy, abuse it, or take it for granted in Jesus's name.
- Father, have mercy on my foundation and blot out forever the sins of my parents and ancestors in Jesus's name.

Overcoming Ignorance

Challenges

- When you really thirst for knowledge.
- When you are fed up with ignorance.
- When you yearn to be self-confident and fearless.

The Word Solution

Ignorance is worse than cancer. It is a terrible disease, one of the most fatal. Sometimes, it is indistinguishable from extreme foolishness. Ignorance is not just not knowing what to do or how to do the right thing; ignorance is a state of living half-empty. An ignorant person can easily be led to the slaughter and may even blissfully but unwittingly put his head on the chopping block. An ignorant person is a disaster waiting to happen. He is easily controlled and manipulated even by his subordinates. God detests ignorance. He is unhappy with its consequences, the perishing of His people (Hosea 4:6) and the captivity of His people (Isaiah 5:13).

Lack of knowledge has driven many to grievous errors and untimely deaths. Some Christians do not know their rights and privileges in Christ. They are unaware of the powers conferred on them to make their captors captives (Revelation 13:10). Some have gone in desperation to consult false priests and false prophets. By that error, they have fallen captive to the devil and have been oppressed, obsessed, or possessed.

The only solution to ignorance is knowledge: "Through knowledge shall the just be delivered" (Proverbs 11:9). Wisdom delivers, and knowledge sets free. Knowledge of God's Word is power. Human beings should live only by God's Word (Matthew 4:4), which is life itself (John 6:63). Study and meditate on the Bible if you want to gain knowledge of your covenant rights.

By reading the Bible, you will discover what hundreds of millions before you have come to know. It is an inexhaustible fountain of living water that quenches all human thirst. Search the scriptures because in them you will find life. Read books and writings by anointed servants of God. Attend Christian fellowships. Fast and pray, and ask God for revelation knowledge. Stop walking in ignorance. You will become a head and no longer be a tail.

The Prayer Solution

- Father, put inside me a hunger and thirst for your Word in Jesus's name.
- Father, please forgive whatever I have done wrong in ignorance, and grant by your mercy that it will not define the rest of my life in Jesus's name.
- Father, do not let me perish for lack of knowledge in Jesus's name.
- Father, teach me to seek right and acquire knowledge of you in Jesus's name.
- May every seed of ignorance in my family perish in Jesus's name.
- Father, connect me with human vessels who are overflowing with the right knowledge in Jesus's name.
- Father, make me a faithful carrier and channel of divine knowledge in Jesus's name.

The Power of Effective Prayers

Challenges

- When you need a revival in your prayer life.
- When you are feeling frustrated and unable to pray.
- When you feel your prayers have yielded no real answers.
- When you wonder how to pray to receive results.

The Word Solution

There is more power in prayer than in all the nuclear arsenals of the world. Its power is limitless. Unfortunately, too many believers are not very serious about praying. Some merely play with it. Others are prone to replacing it with other spiritual exercises such as fasting, praising, tithing, Bible study, or meditation. All these spiritual exercises are excellent and powerful tools, hallmarks of a good Christian's life. They are necessary and beneficial as are regular attendance at church and fellowship with brethren (iron sharpens iron). But none is a substitute for prayer.

A popular church song reminds us that Jesus started and ended with prayer. His earthly ministry began with prayer and fasting in the wilderness. That awesome ministry ended with an all-night prayer vigil in the garden of Gethsemane. But even as He hung dying on the cross, He prayed to God to forgive his killers, who did not know what they were doing.

Every disciple of Jesus must follow the Master's example. The four gospels bear witness that Jesus lived a life of active and regular prayers. He rose early each day long before dawn to pray in a quiet place (Mark 1:35). So important is prayer to God that Jesus took pains to teach His disciples how to pray. He directed us to follow His pattern of prayer and do so with perseverance and determination (Matthew 7:7).

We all need to improve on our attitude toward and disposition to prayer. Enough of casual prayers! Some pray with hands in pockets as if chatting with their mates. Some make and take on their mobile phone while praying. They give themselves over to all manner of distractions right in the act of prayer. Roaming eyes and minds lust after physical vanities such as what others are wearing. Some fall asleep and snore. You would not indulge in such discourteous acts while talking to anyone you had respect for, so why would you treat God that way?

Prayer is a petition to God, and the intensity of your prayer indicates how desperate you are to move God to answer you as quickly as possible. Recall the plea of blind Bartimaeus and the ten lepers who came to Jesus crying for mercy. If you desire God to intervene in your situation, why would you mumble a few prayers for a few minutes and expect radical results? Jesus asked the apostles to pray with Him for at least an hour.

The effectual, fervent prayer of a righteous man avails much (James 5:16). If you want your prayer to avail much, put fervency in it and live a righteous life. It is a combination of virtues guaranteed to produce the best for you. Friend, restore your broken altar of prayer.

The Prayer Solution

- I know not how to pray, but Father, by Your Spirit, teach me how to pray in Jesus's name.
- Father, wake me up from slumber and complacency. Help me revive my prayer life in Jesus's name.
- Lord Jesus, as you prayed for Simon Peter, please pray for me so I will not fall away from you.
- Father, Job prayed for others and his captivity was turned around. Teach me how to pray unselfish prayers in Jesus's name.
- Father, give me the grace to fast in time of need in Jesus's name.
- Father, lead me through your Word and guide me in applying it in prayer in Jesus's name.
- Father, strengthen me in fervent prayers that avail much in Jesus's name.

Corporate Anointing

Challenges

- When for too long you have prayed alone but have received no solution.
- When you desire greater access to God's power.

The Word Solution

Many years ago, I read a book by Kenneth Hagin; he devoted a chapter to what he called corporate anointing, spiritual energy that comes into effect when people come together to worship God. Jesus declared that when two or more were gathered in His name, He would be in their midst.

A gathering of people in honor of Jesus attracts His presence. There is therefore a corporate anointing in the gathering of God's people.

On the day of Pentecost, the Holy Spirit came down on the gathering of Christ's disciples. He could quite easily have visited them one by one, but He visited them when they were in the Upper Room. There is power in unity of purpose as a hallmark of the body of Christ. It is why we are advised not to forsake the assembly of believers (Hebrews 10:25). Anyone who keeps away from church fellowship is only denying himself the profound benefits of corporate anointing.

In the Old Testament, God often asked the leaders of His people to call a solemn assembly (Joel 2:15). God would arrive as His people were assembled in His honor, and the glory of His presence would be evident in signs and wonders.

There is no doubt that God could heal a sick person in the privacy of his own bedroom. One can even be healed while alone listening to Christian radio or watching a Christian program on TV or a webcast. God can and does heal everywhere, but so much more is wrought by the corporate anointing that flows from His tangible presence in the gathering of His people. As a believer, you owe it to yourself, to God, and to your fellow believers to be a part of such gatherings. If God can touch you separately in your remote place of solitude, how much more can He do if you are part of His congregation?

It takes your physical presence to benefit from corporate anointing. Never miss out on Christian fellowship you are meant to be part of or a church program you are supposed to attend. Your miracle is waiting for you in the congregation of the brethren.

The Prayer Solution

- Father, wherever I go, position me in the congregation of believers and let me receive your divine touch always in Jesus's name.
- Father, dismantle every power hindering my regular attendance at Christian fellowships and church in Jesus's name.
- Father, may your presence be evident at any congregational meeting of believers I attend or belong to in Jesus's name.

- Father, use me and mine to gather people for the release of your corporate anointing in Jesus's name.
- Father, never let me forsake the assembly of believers in Jesus's name.
- Father, may your presence be an abiding feature of worship in my church in Jesus's name.
- Father, please give me every resource I need for regular attendance in the assembly of believers in Jesus's name.

The Power of Holiness

Challenges

- When you want blessings in abundance
- When you want swift and regular answer to your prayers.
- When you want God fighting for you.
- When you want to live a sinless and healthy life.

The Word Solution

Many Christians believe erroneously that all their problems come from witches, wizards, and occult powers. A number wrongly believe that the solution to their minutest problem lies in fiery prayer and lengthy fasts. Gearing up for twenty-one days of prayer and fasting or seven days of nonstop vigil has become a common habit in Christendom. This is increasingly making Christianity seem far more complex and difficult than it is. Everywhere these days is a siege and fear mentality that unwittingly tends to magnify the devil. "It is finished" were Jesus's final words at Calvary. He won salvation, victory, and divine favor for all humankind. Christians receive these by faith in Christ and His grace, not by their works or power and might.

When faced with problems and challenges, many fail to consider their personal standing with God. Honest self-assessment is a must for every Christian. What medical treatment can be reasonably administered to a patient without a prior proper checkup? Before you rush into a marathon of fasting and warrior praying, undergo a spiritual self-scanning to accurately diagnose your condition. Are you holy, or have you fallen into sin? God does not open His ears to the prayers of sinners or stretch out His hands to help them (Isaiah 59:1–2).

Ask yourself about your own standing with God. The Holy Spirit will readily assist you in that exercise if with humility and sincerity you ask Him to convict you of your sins. Anyone who loves secret sins cannot prosper (Proverbs 28:13). If you are in sin, the hedge around you is broken (Ecclesiastes 10:8) and witches and wizards can attack you. If you remain unrepentant, even if the evil forces are cast away, they will return with higher demons.

Back to the basics … Repentance is key to reconciliation with God. Repent now and forsake sins. You cannot commit adultery and at the same time pray to God to heal your marriage. Get back to holiness and you will receive the mercies of God. Praying to God should feel more like a young lad's pleasant conversation with his loving father; a few short requests can bring swift answers.

I am looking forward to your testimonies.

The Prayer Solution

- Father, I have sinned against you. I have broken your Commandments and transgressed your laws. May I receive grace this moment to confess all my sins and renounce them in Jesus's name.
- Father, I ask for total forgiveness of my sins. I ask for your mercy. Wash away my sins with the precious blood of Jesus.
- Father, please heal me of every pain or sorrow resulting from my sin in Jesus's name.
- Father, grant me your grace to overcome every temptation ever again to sin against you in Jesus's name.
- Father, give me the grace to live a holy life that is acceptable to you in Jesus's name.
- Father, absolve me of and deliver me from any guilt I inherited from my parents and ancestors by Jesus's blood in Jesus's name.
- Father, please restore the hedge of protection my sin against you has weakened or broken in Jesus's name.

- Father, bless me with the blessings of holiness as promised by your Word in Jesus's name.
- I, a child of God washed clean by the blood of Jesus, command every enemy blocking my way to be cast out now in Jesus's name.
- As a redeemed of the Lord washed clean by the precious blood of Jesus, I reclaim my full rights as a son of God to live a holy life. I will exercise the power of God over my problems in Jesus's name.

A New Thing

Challenges

- When you are at a dead end yet stuck with old things.
- When you are craving a total change.
- When you need new doors to be opened for you.
- When you yearn for a new direction.
- When your need for drastic improvement has become an emergency.

The Word Solution

The beginning of a new thing implies the end of an old thing. In most cases, a new thing is an improvement on an old thing, and it brings joy.

God said He would do "a new thing" (Isaiah 43:18–19). It is a simple statement, but loads of benefits are attached to it by the explicit elaboration that follows. The almighty God will make a way in the wilderness—a safe and convenient passage through seemingly impossible situations you find yourself in. He will make rivers flow in the desert for you; you will have ample provisions for your life journey. No matter how difficult the circumstances on the road ahead are, you will have God's assurance that He can and will take care of you. He will make every impossible thing possible for His trusting child. That should be cheering news for anyone passing through an extremely tough situation that seems there is no way out of. God is about to make you a winner. Go in faith. Rivers in the desert will quench your thirst and water the ground for planting. A new era of fruitfulness is on your horizon to perfect the total transformation only our God can bring about.

Become part of that glorious transformation today. Expect fruitfulness and increase by receiving the flow of the Holy Spirit, the power that opens doors in impossible places. Your miracle is waiting for you in any difficult challenge. Ask God to do a new thing in your life today.

The Prayer Solution

- Father, in your merciful kindness, set right everything the enemy has disorganized in my family in Jesus's name.
- Father, I am weary of songs of pain and sorrow; please give me a new song of joy in Jesus's name.
- Father, command a new beginning for me, a new dawn of fruitfulness and abundant life in Jesus's name.
- May I gladly let go of whatever is past, used, or overdue for replacement, Father, in Jesus's name. Father, renew my mind in every aspect of life so I can put you first in all things in Jesus's name.
- Father, cause me to infect anyone I meet with a new song of your goodness and a new zeal for you in Jesus's name.
- Father, as you open new doors for me, may I receive grace not only to enter but also to share the open doors with others in Jesus's name.

Rivers in the Desert

Challenges

- When the impossible must be made possible.
- When a completely hopeless situation must be reversed.
- When no human solution is conceivable or within reach.
- When natural limitations must be set aside.

The Word Solution

Water is rare and thus precious in deserts. Oases have become places of human settlement for that reason. A flowing river is an impossibility in a desert; it is futile to search for one anywhere as the place would not be a desert if a river were there. Only God could make a river in a desert; it would be a new thing as Bible records (Isaiah 43:19). But His ways are unsearchable. He drew water out of the jawbone of a donkey for a thirsty and dehydrated Samson (Judges 15:16, 19). He caused water to spring from a rock in the wilderness for a whole nation (Exodus 17:1–7).

God's promise to you is expressly stated. He will cause rivers to flow in the desert for your sake. Every dry place that looks like a desert in your life will receive a flow of life-giving water from heaven. God will pour forth blessings as torrents that flow like great rivers. Impossible things will become possible, and the irreversible will be reversed. Natural limitations will give way to the supernatural, and God's will miraculously provide for those who are in bad shape.

Our God is the great provider. Our Lord Jesus is the giver of abundant life (John 10:10). He promised to give us much more than we could ever ask for or imagine (Ephesians 3:20). Not a small stream but a mighty river He will cause to flow in your desert.

Some years ago, I worked as the regional head of a medium-sized bank. There weren't many big-name clients because commercial enterprises and manufacturing companies were few in the area, and none of the big-money conglomerates had a presence in the region. Hitting the sales target was not humanly possible in that virtual financial desert, but contrary to human logic, statistics, and projections, that region soon became the most profitable one in the bank's business. It beat all others including those in commercial capitals as well as those in rich oil and gas hubs. It was a supernatural performance that stood for two years. The secret was prayer and fasting in a life of holiness and diligence at work. I am a living witness that God causes rivers to flow in the desert.

What about you? Are you stranded in the middle of a desert and in need of a river of blessings? Simply commit to living a holy life and ask God for your rivers of living water. God is ready. You will be amazed at His miracles, His new beginnings. Welcome to a manifestation of the supernatural in your favor, rivers flowing in every desert place of your life. Congratulations!

The Prayer Solution

- Father, command rivers into every desert of my life in Jesus's name.
- Father, I have asked in faith for things I know are humanly impossible. I trust you to make them possible in Jesus's name.
- Father, do a new thing in my family—relieve the stress and lighten the burden for every one of us in Jesus's name.
- In your great mercy, Father, reverse every affliction or reproach that seems irreversible in my life today in Jesus's name.
- Father, remove every natural limitation in my life in your omnipotence in Jesus's name.

Chapter 8

Capsules for Divine Healing

Power of Forgiveness

Challenges

- When it feels that God does not hear your prayers.
- When nothing is going right and you are all questions and no answers.
- When you need peace of mind and forgiveness from God and humanity.
- When your heart is filled with bitterness and pain.

The Word Solution

Pastor Adeboye once told an interesting story about a rich widower whose daughter was his only child. The girl's mother had died young, and the widower naturally lavished much love and care on their only child. Before giving her in marriage, he extracted a special commitment from his son-in-law, a pledge to take exceptional care of his special daughter.

However, the son-in-law did not keep his promise; he mistreated his young bride and often beat her up. When the rich man found that out, he vowed never to forgive his impertinent son-in-law. Not long after, he fell very ill. In spite of best efforts, no doctor could diagnose or cure his illness. He sought help from men of God, but God restrained His various servants from praying for him. A pastor told him to forgive anyone who had gravely offended him. The rich father-in-law visited his son-in-law and embraced him. To the glory of God, he was healed of that illness.

Has someone hurt you so deeply that you cannot forgive him or her? Are you nursing bitterness or malice against anyone? Unforgiveness is a yoke of bondage (Matthew 18:35). The Lord Jesus taught us how to pray, and a key element in His model of prayer is the request to God to forgive our offenses as we forgive those who have offended us (Luke 11:4). Jesus warned that whoever bears causeless anger against his brother will be judged to have committed the same offense as outright murder (Matthew 5:21–22).

Look closely at your relationships with family, friends, associates, neighbors, and fellow church members. Do you resent any of them? Are you struggling with bitterness or hatred toward anyone but doing a good job of keeping up appearances?

Some of your prayers may be answered only when you have honestly dealt with issues of bitterness and unforgiveness in your heart. People may truly have wronged you, treated you badly, conspired against you, dealt unfairly with you, troubled you, or sabotaged your best efforts. Some may have rewarded your goodness to them with evil. That is not new; it is exactly what happened to Jesus, but He graciously asked His Father to forgive those who persecuted Him (Luke 23:24).

You can tap into the unbelievable power in forgiveness. It takes a high level of maturity and humility to let go of hurts or malice. You cannot claim to be humble in spirit if you cannot forgive an offense. Unforgiveness is spiritual bondage that blocks your vision and hinders your breakthrough, and it could afflict you with a demon of sickness from which there is no deliverance unless you forgive and let go. Show forgiveness today, terminate malice, and the enemy will lose all legal grounds to afflict you.

Forgive. We will soon hear your testimonies to the glory of God.

The Prayer Solution

- Father, give me the grace to forgive those who hurt me in Jesus's name.
- Father, as I have forgiven those who have hurt me, please forgive my sins in Jesus's name.

- Father because I bear no grudge against anyone, please deliver me from all forms of bondage in Jesus's name.
- Father, please show me your goodness and mercy and extend the same to my family in Jesus's name.
- Father, release on me all the blessings that follow a forgiving spirit in Jesus's name.
- Father, teach me to be quick to forgive at all times in Jesus's name.
- Father, help me to be more sensitive to causing than to taking offense. May I always avoid offending or provoking others in Jesus's name.

The Power of Holy Communion

Challenges

- When you strongly desire the Passover experience.
- When you desire freedom from bondage or healing of sickness.
- When you want deliverance from oppression, repression, or suppression.
- When you need an unforgettable restoration.
- When you want God's judgment of your enemies.
- When you desire the physical touch of God.
- When your problems have defied your prayers.

The Word Solution

Some Christians have never tapped into the illimitable powers of Holy Communion. Indeed, quite a lot see Holy Communion as just another Christian ritual that is carried out to achieve righteousness. A great number do not even partake in Holy Communion. Contributing significantly to their unfortunate indifference is the lack of emphasis by the clergy on the subject. There is also the matter of doctrinal errors by some church denominations regarding this sacred ordinance. It has bred confusion and affected many for the worse. Some good folks are put off by the controversies, and others have reacted to perceived fakery by ditching the whole rite completely.

But Holy Communion is indeed the very essence of the Passover instituted by God Himself (Exodus 12:1–51). It is a divinely ordered feast signifying God's everlasting covenant of deliverance for His people. To eat of it is a divine privilege reserved for the elect. Partakers feast on God's leaven of faith and eternal life, healing, and rejuvenation. It is a leaven of deliverance, a crossover banquet that nourishes its partakers to go in strength after his destiny. It is a meal of the highest favor. But it is also a meal of death if taken unworthily (1 Corinthians 11:30).

Jesus is the Bread of Life, and nobody who does not eat His body and drink His blood can gain everlasting life (John 6:53). Holy Communion is the symbol of His body and blood. We are mandated as His followers to take it as often as possible in memory of Him.

The first Holy Communion was the Lord's last meal with His twelve apostles. It was in commemoration of the Passover, the great night of God's deliverance of His people from bondage in Egypt. The Passover in Egypt involved the slaying and eating of an unblemished lamb by every household. In the Last Supper, Jesus offered Himself as the Lamb slain for the entire household of God and for all time. He gave His apostles bread and wine as tokens of His body that would be broken and blood that would be shed for the remission of sins. In Egypt, it took the covenantal blood of a lowly animal to provoke God's awesome move that shook Pharaoh's kingdom to its foundations. How much more now is our faithful appreciation of a superior covenant in the precious blood of His only begotten Son!

You must have heard hundreds of amazing testimonies about Holy Communion and its showers of blessings that fell on devout communicants. There have been from age to age endless accounts and records of incredible healings, amazing restoration, miraculous deliverances, and other supernatural interventions. Holy Communion taken in faith represents and delivers the living presence and power of Jesus Christ in His church of yesterday, today, and forever.

Are you battling with any ostensibly impossible problem? Is there anything that God through His Son cannot do? At a Holy Communion service in my former parish, a man testified of his healing from heart failure. At another, a pregnant woman whose baby was breech received supernatural repositioning of her baby. Not long after, she went into labor for just a few minutes and delivered with the ease of the Hebrew women.

Present your challenges to God on the altar of Holy Communion. You will be glad for God's unfailing intervention.

The Prayer Solution

- Father, by the blood of Jesus present in Holy Communion, wash me clean and flush out every form of diseases from my blood in Jesus's name.
- Father, honor my faith as I partake of Holy Communion and cause your covenant power to manifest in me in Jesus's name.
- Father, by taking Holy Communion, I connect by faith to your night of Passover in Egypt, and by this token of blood, I ask that every yoke in my life be summarily destroyed in Jesus's name.
- Father, by your bruised and broken body, I receive healing in Jesus's name.
- Father, by Holy Communion, I am joined to you and therefore completely separated from the works of Satan in Jesus's name.
- Lord Jesus, I confess you as the Bread of Life. Feed me till I want no more.
- Father, preserve me in holiness and purity of spirit that in worthiness I may always partake in Holy Communion in Jesus's name.

Overcoming Sicknesses and Diseases

Challenges

- When you are troubled with sicknesses.
- When drugs disappoint you and your hope of healing is left shaky or fading.
- When you realize your sickness is demon inspired.

The Word Solution

Sickness is neither good for anyone nor meant for the children of God. It comes mostly as an affliction from the devil or as a consequence of an individual's acts of commission or omission—eating with unwashed hands, drinking impure water, or failing to protect your house against mosquitoes. Malaria due to mosquito bites and typhoid fever due to unsanitary environments are direct consequences of personal faults and failures.

Sicknesses are in the arsenal of the age-old devil; they are wicked, unsparing torments that he fires at will against the children of God. But the almighty God has reserved healing for His beloved children. Healing is their food, and God is their trusted wall of defense. When they live holy lives, Satan cannot breach God's special fortress of ample provisions and total protection for them.

You dwell there by right as a favored child of God, and you have God's assurance that you will never lose that state unless you yield to the devil's temptation and fall into sin, which God abhors. Anyone who sins presents Satan with an opening in God's protective hedge for a direct attack. The evil one will gladly seize that opening to afflict someone with sickness and pain (Deuteronomy 28:60–61).

Are you facing a health challenge that is not responding to medical treatment? Is there an unconfessed sin in your heart? Are you laboring under the burden of guilt or a pricking of conscience reminding you of your secret faults? You need to face up to your situation. Godly sorrow works repentance to salvation (2 Corinthians 7:10). Go before God with a contrite spirit, confess your sins, and ask for His forgiveness. God will not reject a broken and contrite spirit (Psalm 51:17). With your sins forgiven and blotted out, expect your perfect healing as you ask God for it. He denies you nothing you ask for in faith.

There is a direct link between faith and healing. Those who came to Jesus for healing had to declare their personal faith in His power to heal their conditions. Jesus habitually credited His miraculous healing to His supplicant's declared faith in Him (Mark 5:34; Luke 8:48; Luke 17:19). That faith must be anchored on the Word of God as amply laid down in the scriptures (1 Peter 2:25; Exodus 15:26; Psalms 103:3, 107:20; Isaiah 53:5; Jeremiah 30:17). A life lived believing and confessing these scriptures is a life of victorious power over every sickness and disease. He who promised this is God, the almighty and everlasting Father who never fails.

Receive your healing today—total healing for your body, soul, and spirit.

The Prayer Solution

- Every genealogical sickness in my life I reject and terminate forever in Jesus's name.
- Every sickness projected into my life by any power be nullified and reversed in Jesus's name.
- Every tree of sickness planted in my life be uprooted in Jesus's name.
- Every curse of infirmity in my family be broken in Jesus's name.
- By Jesus's stripes, I receive healing and deliverance from every infirmity in Jesus's name.
- Sickness and disease depart from my body and never come back in Jesus's name.
- Father, you are the Lord who heals me. May I celebrate you in perfect health of mind and body all the days of my life in Jesus's name.

Chapter 9

Capsules for Peace of Mind

Power of Inner Peace

Challenges

- When you lack peace of mind.
- When you have sleepless nights.
- When in the eyes of men you seem successful but inside you is emptiness.
- When you lack contentment.
- When you keep searching for solutions to indefinable problems.
- When you keep suffering emotional breakdown.

The Word Solution

I once visited a very wealthy man, an elderly friend who loved chatting with me. On one occasion, I found him strangely withdrawn and moody, and I asked him what was wrong. His reply was instant and shocking: "There is no peace for the wicked," he blurted out before he realized that by his own lips he was creating problems for himself.

Of course, he made efforts to reverse or revise his words, but all his further speechmaking was an obvious exercise in futility; the truth was out. He was a troubled man who like Shakespeare's Macbeth had murdered sleep and would sleep no more. His façade of cultivated ease, comfort, and wealth was all fake. Behind it was a reality of disquiet and distress. He had no peace. That was the truth he had programmed himself to conceal permanently, but there it was by reflex out in the open; out of the abundance of the heart, the mouth speaks (Luke 6:45).

Most people wrongly believe that peace and joy are to be found in the lifestyles of the rich and opulent. Their sights are set eternally on million-dollar cars and yachts, mansions of gold, expensive dressing, exotic foods, and pricey world travel, luxury resorts, and billionaire club getaways. The truth is that none of these things can give you peace of mind. Joy and inner peace cannot be bought with money. It is a gift of God reserved for His own. In case you are wondering why anyone needs it or what real use it can be to you, the answer is incontrovertible. If you lack inner peace, you feel under siege all day, and at sunset, there is little hope of respite as you may not have a good night's rest. For most people in that troubled condition, sleep may come only with the help of pills. It is a life of intense fears and worries, and very often, the result is high blood pressure with its countless complications. Without inner peace, no one can have the presence of mind and sense of balance to live right and help others live right. You cannot relate well with others much less with God. You cannot even pray correctly if you manage to pray at all. You are at war with yourself and everybody else.

Inner peace proceeds from contentment, and it breeds more contentment. Whoever lacks it may be driven to endless strife and bitter rivalry by insatiable greed or other unnatural impulses. Such a person is a danger to himself and others. He is a ready tool in the hands of the devil. He cannot hear or understand God's assuring words such as, "Come unto me, all ye that labor and are heavy laden and I will give you rest" (Matthew 11:28–29) and "Cast all your care upon Him for He careth for you" (1 Peter 5:7). These are covenant words meant to enliven our faith in God as a caring Father who knows all our cares big and small.

One evening in 2010 while I was a volunteer full-time worker in a church, I had a deep desire to eat beans prepared in my preferred way. On getting home, I had a pleasant surprise—that was the dish my wife had prepared. I smiled at her, and she asked what made me smile. When I told her that the meal she had prepared was my exact desire, she did not show any surprise as she had her own story—a gentle voice had urged her while she had been napping that afternoon to prepare beans for dinner for me.

Friend, God cares about everything you care about. The inner peace you need as a human being is important to your Maker too. He is the owner and giver of it, so go to Him, the Prince of Peace (Isaiah 9:16). He is inviting you personally by His loving overture: "My peace I give to you" (John 14:27). Turn to your Savior, Jesus, the owner and dispenser of peace. Trust in and live by His Word and His Holy Spirit will live in you and make you His friend and joint heir of God's kingdom riches. Seek His peace. He will give you the peace that passes all understanding.

The Prayer Solution

- Lord Jesus, come into my heart; I make you Lord and Savior of my life. Reign in my life from now on even to the end of my days, amen.
- Father, I surrender to your authority and government from today on; rule in all my affairs without exception in Jesus's name.
- Father, give me the gift of godliness and contentment, and may I never be ruled by greed or inordinate desires in Jesus's name.
- Father, give me peace that passes all understanding in Jesus's name.
- Prince of Peace, manifest your presence in all my relationships and endeavors in Jesus's name.
- Father, may I walk in divine wisdom and never lose your peace in Jesus's name.
- Father, may I remain a channel of your peace in Jesus's name.

Comfort in Tribulation

Challenges

- When you cannot understand why you are undergoing difficult times.
- When you are feeling dispirited despite your holiness.
- When you feel helpless because friends and close relations are suffering tribulations.
- When every day is full of misery, pain, and sorrow.

The Word Solution

There is this common notion that once you become a born-again Christian, all your problems will fizzle away. It is a false teaching, but regrettably, too many have bought into it. They need to learn the hard truth that even good Christians suffer lots of physical afflictions. Living a holy life does not make you immune to life's troubles.

One side effect of the wrong teaching is the tendency of many Christians to wrongfully impute sin as the cause of every sickness or trial anyone is going through. Even ailing fellow Christians are not spared the insensitive and unscriptural prejudice of those who believe that every tribulation is a recompense for sin. But if no holy person can ever be attacked by the devil, what about Job, a man who was "perfect and upright, and one that feared God, and eschewed evil"? (Job 1:1). What sin did he commit? God, not man, certified Job holy and righteous. He was a man who prayed for himself and for his children and made sacrifices for their sins if any. Yet Satan struck at him and his family.

David, king and prophet, was divinely gifted with revelation of spiritual truth of life on this earth up to the hereafter. One of his most explicit declarations about human sufferings is that "many are the afflictions of the righteous" (Psalm 34:19). Our Lord and Savior made it clear to His disciples that in this world, they would have tribulations (John 16:33). Note the implicit assurances in the happy ending of both scriptures—the righteous would be delivered from all their afflictions, and Christ's disciples should be of good cheer because Christ had overcome the world on their behalf.

The apostle Paul told us that the suffering of the righteous had a divine purpose; it revealed God as the Father of mercies and the God of all comfort who comforts us in all our tribulation. And it equips us to empathize with others and to comfort them in the same way and manner that God comforted us in our times of distress (2 Corinthians 1:3–4).

Good friend, tribulation in this world is not reserved for the unrighteous. The wind blows against all, and the rain falls on the good and the evil alike; tribulations befall saints and sinners. The only difference is that God has an assured plan of deliverance for His saints: "Though you pass through the waters, the flood will not overflow you and when you pass through the fire, it will not kindle upon you" (Isaiah 43:2). It is for this reason that the just will live by faith (Romans 1:17, Galatians 3:11, Hebrews 10:38), faith that it will be well (Isaiah 3:10), faith that all things work together for good for those who love God (Romans 8:28), faith that the terrors you are seeing this moment will be seen no more (Exodus 14:13, 2 Corinthians 4:17), and faith that weeping might endure for a night but joy will come in the morning (Psalm 30:5) Fear and anxiety about any situation are enemies of faith, and they are forbidden ground for the righteous.

It is our Christian duty to show love always and particularly to those in distress or grief. We must comfort one another in tribulation (2 Corinthians 1:4). We must avoid hasty suppositions and prejudicial verdicts against our fellow human beings in their time of trouble when they need us most.

The Prayer Solution

- Father, cause me to remember always that though I pass through the fire, it will never burn me because you will deliver me according to your Word.
- Father, cause me to keep in mind that though I pass through the flood, I will not drown for you are with me by your covenant of promise.
- Father, I thank you that you have gone ahead of me. You have positioned help, encouragement, and support for me in the way that I must go.
- Father, make me an intercessor for people in tribulation and especially those suffering for the sake of your name in Jesus's name.
- Father, give me the grace to overcome challenges and come out better as a comforter and encourager of others in Jesus's name.
- Father, never let my faith falter or fail in times of trial in Jesus's name.
- Father, be my comfort always unto faith testimonies in Jesus's name.

All Will Be Well

Challenges

- When you feel sick and tired in body, soul, and spirit.
- When you are depressed unto death.
- When you feel down and out, helpless, and hopeless.
- When all around you is gloom and failure.
- When your thoughts are turning grim and almost suicidal.

The Word Solution

"And God saw everything that he had made; and, behold, it was very good" (Genesis 1:31). That was the state of the world at creation. Everything God made was well made. Man was never sick, nor did he lack anything. He enjoyed regular fellowship with his Maker, who gave him dominion over all creation. Then man blew it by the sin of disobedience that entered through Adam. Sickness, suffering, sorrow, and death followed as components of the curse on sinful man (Genesis 3:17).

But God would show mercy by sending His Son to die on the cross to free humanity from that curse. The Lord Jesus took the place of all humankind on the cross; He, a sinless man, died for the sins of all people and redeemed them from every curse (Galatians 3:13–14). All ordinances that were previously against us were nailed to the cross of Jesus (Colossians 2:14). Through Jesus, we have total redemption from our sins as He provided grace (John 1:17). Help came from above and restored hope and brought us salvation. Jesus came to give us abundant life (John 10:10), and by His finished work, He reversed all the works of the devil (1 John 3:8).

God's wish is that all will be well with you. His thoughts for you are thoughts of peace, not of evil, to give you an expected end (Jeremiah 29:11).

In 2012, my first daughter was facing a challenge with math during her final year in high school. My wife tried in vain to help her tackle a difficult homework problem. I too stepped in but failed as well. The three of us went to bed frustrated and unhappy. In sleep that night, I received from God a step-by-step solution to the problem. I woke up, and following the revealed procedure, we solved in two minutes a problem that had defied our joint efforts for over three hours. God proved Himself once again in my situation. He is my helper and enabler, a Father worthy of all my trust. He is aware of anything that worries me, even mundane things such as my daughter's math problem. He can deal with them to ensure me that all is well with me.

Be assured, good friend, that all will be well with you in Jesus's name. All you need to make it happen is Jesus. Receive Him today as your Savior, and make Him your ally in all you do or plan to do. He will guide and settle you into a new life of righteousness with its attendant blessings. It was written about those blessings, "Say ye to the righteous that it shall be well with him: for they shall eat the fruit of their doings" (Isaiah 3:10). Your every seed as a righteous man or woman will bear good fruit, and you will eat thereof.

What seed are you sowing, and what seed did you sow in the past? Sow a righteous seed and you will eat righteous fruit. All will be well because God Himself promised that.

The Prayer Solution

- Father, mercifully blot out my transgressions and renew a right spirit in me in Jesus's name.
- Restore all that the enemy has stolen, killed, or destroyed in my life, Father, in Jesus's name.
- Father, help me shun all crooked ways and walk only the straight and narrow path to my destiny in Jesus's name.
- Father, renew my strength of body, soul, and spirit in Jesus's name.
- Father, cause every good seed I have sown to yield a bountiful harvest in Jesus's name.
- Father, help me live a life that appreciates your divine assurance that all will be well with the righteous in Jesus's name.

Overcoming Fear

Challenges

- When you live in danger or constant fear.
- When you are facing threats, intimidation, and harassment.
- When you are battling extreme doubt or uncertainty.

The Word Solution

Fear is the opposite of faith. Without faith, no one can please God (Hebrews 11:6). Without faith in yourself, fear can take over your life and the devil can take hold of you. The devil uses fear to submit human beings to his evil program. Fear is a major weapon he wields to subdue and subjugate his captives in tyrant chains and cells of oppression, suppression, repression, and obsession. Fear is not of God because God has not given us the spirit of fear but of power and of love and sound mind (2 Timothy 1:7). That is why the righteous are as bold as lions (Proverbs 28:1).

God never sends fear to His children. Angels He sent in dreams or trances greeted His friends with assuring words—"Fear not." Bible scholars have counted 366 mentions of "Fear not" in the Bible, one for every day of the year plus one for leap years.

One way to overcome fear is by realizing and appreciating who you are in Christ Jesus. If you knew you were the offspring of the Lion of Judah (hence a lion in your own right), what would you fear? If you knew you were a king and a priest (Revelation 5:10), whom would you fear? If you knew you were more than a conqueror (Romans 8:37), why would you fear? If you knew you were a royal priesthood (1 Peter 2:9), whom would you be afraid of?

The strongest reason to not fear is not you but rather He who is in you; He is greater than any power in the world (1 John 4:4), and He has promised never to leave you or forsake you (Hebrews 13:5). He says no one can pluck you out of His hands (John 10:28).

I used to be afraid at night many years ago. I was constantly tormented in sleep by nightmares that made me fear imaginary stalkers and unseen attackers. My fear disappeared when God opened my eyes one night to see angels on guard around me. I woke up to a fuller understanding of God's delightful assurance that He had ordered His angels to guard me (Psalm 91:11).

Cast out your spirit of fear. The beauty of your destiny in Christ is the assured victory that is reserved for every true Christian. No matter what the devil tries to do, you will always win in the end. Panic, suspense, and fear are only for those who are unsure of the outcome of a contest. God has made you a winner in the contest over your life's issues, a victory determined and declared ahead of the battles. If the Lord is for you, who can be against you? (Romans 8:31). Tell Satan to shut up. Face him down with faith and confidence of who you are in Christ. You are a son of God by the blood of Jesus. Resist the devil and he will flee from you (James 4:7).

There are many forms of spiritual conflicts. Some are so intense that they involve demonic physical manifestations. Are you confronted with such a conflict—all sorts of unimaginable horrors coming at you from every corner? Are you living in dread that you are going out of your mind? Friend, stand firm on the Word of God. It is your only way to claim the victory Jesus has ordered for you. Walk by faith, not by sight (2 Corinthians 5:7) because what you see is deceitful and passing away, but God's Word is the Rock of Ages. Stand on that Rock and confess by faith that you will never again see the terrors you see today (Exodus 14:13). God honors faith in His Word to the point that even your own command spoken in faith will move mountains (Mark 11:34). Put all your trust in God and cast out fear and doubt, for with God, all things are possible (Mark 10:27).

I see you walking in victorious faith from this day on.

The Prayer Solution

- Father, strengthen my faith in you in Jesus's name.
- Father, help me to know who I am in you in Jesus's name.
- I renounce and cast out every spirit of fear in me in Jesus's name.
- Father, help me resolve to walk by faith and not by sight in Jesus's name.

- Father, renew my mind by your Holy Spirit as I study and meditate on your Word in Jesus's name.
- Father, teach me to place absolute trust in you always in Jesus's name.

Waiting for the Promise

Challenges

- When pressure is unbearable and further waiting seems pointless.
- When time is running out and patience has not yielded any results.
- When God is slow or late in meeting His promise to you.
- When you feel left out while others are receiving God's favors.

The Word Solution

A few days ago at morning prayer with my household, I was prompted to teach my children the big difference between magic and miracles. They had been perplexed by my remark that God performed miracles while the devil performed magic. To illustrate my point, I used a handy object that was clearly purple in color. I made my young ones realize that the devil is quite adept at creating illusions. He could make that same purple object appear sooty black but only for a second. That is magic, an experience that is illusory and deceitful unlike God's miracles, which are real and reliable. Magic is instant whereas miracles may come in stages. For example, if God were to change the color of that object, the process would most likely be gradual and take hours, days, or even weeks.

An inescapable fact of life is the test of time that is waiting for every creature. All the works and happenings on this earth must pass or fail that test be they good or bad. The devil's instant magic fades quickly while God's miracles might take ages, but they will abide to His glory. As is written, whatever God does, it will be forever (Ecclesiastes 3:14).

An English proverb says that the mill of the Lord grinds slowly but surely. Ezekiel, His prophet, could easily have been given a straightforward commission to awaken the bones in the valley, but God led him through a step-by-step process for that assignment. First, He caused him to pass by them in contemplation. Next, He got him to command them to hear the Word of God—a necessary preface to the instructions he was about to give the lifeless bones. Their power to hear thus restored, Ezekiel was then made to declare first that breath would enter them and they would live. Second, sinew, flesh, and skin came upon them and they knew God was the Lord. Then, by God's mandate, Ezekiel summoned the winds to breathe life upon them. Though this miracle unfolded in stages, God was busy all the time transforming the bleached bones of a defeated nation into a great army (Ezekiel 37:1–10).

Miracles may appear to take time, but God is gracious and never fails. What miracles are you trusting God for? What answer to a prayer have you had to wait for and has made you worry that God was taking too much time? Be assured that He who made the promise is faithful and cannot fail. His promises are stamped and sealed in Christ Jesus. He has never promised and failed as He is not a man that He should lie (Numbers 23:19).

Have you noticed that the longer the wait, the bigger the miracle? Think of those women in the Bible who suffered many years of childlessness who ended up giving birth to special figures. Samson's mother was called barren (Judges 13:2) as was Joseph's mother, Rachael (Genesis 30:22–24), and Elizabeth, the mother of John the Baptist even though she was married to a priest (Luke 1:7). Samuel, the great judge of Israel, was born after his mother had endured many years of mockery and reproach for her supposed barrenness (1 Samuel 1:7).

Your miracles may be slow in coming, but rest assured they are on the way. God is capable of delivering on every promise He makes. His word about you will come to pass as will every word of the Bible you receive in faith and every prayer you pray in line with His will.

God will deliver. He is not limited by time or space. So wait on Him and He will renew your strength (Isaiah 40:31).

The Prayer Solution

- Father, give me special grace to wait on you always in Jesus's name.
- Father, help my unbelief and teach me to trust you more in Jesus's name.
- Father, teach me to know that your time is the best in Jesus's name.
- Father, for every long wait I have to bear in life, mercifully imbue me with patience and right attitude to you and to others in Jesus's name.
- Please compensate me for any long wait I have to bear in life, Father, with your great abundance in Jesus's name.
- Father, renew my strength as I wait on you in Jesus's name.
- Let me learn whatever I need to learn from any wait, Father, in Jesus's name.
- Father, teach me to do your will always so that my act of commission or omission does not cause a delay in receiving your blessings in Jesus's name.

Chapter 10

Marriage Capsules

Bone of My Bone

Challenges

- When you are anxious to get married.
- When you cannot understand a long wait for marriage.
- When being single has become a challenge if not a reproach.
- When you wonder if it is your fate to remain single.

The Word Solution

Marriage is a mystery (Ephesians 5:31–32). God created man as His masterpiece of creation (Genesis 1:26), But after looking him over, He declared, "It is not good that the man should be alone" (Genesis 2:18). That was His rationale for instituting marriage, a divine union by which man as husband is provided with woman as wife. By this union, husband and wife find perfect helpers and companions in each other.

God is happy whenever a marriage takes place. It was no accident that Jesus started His public ministry at a wedding ceremony and performed a miracle there (John 2:1–10).

Marriage makes a man complete. Adam proclaimed Eve the bone of his bone and the flesh of his flesh (Genesis 2:23). I had no idea how incomplete I was until I got married. Everything I lacked as a human being was packaged for me in my wife. She arrived bringing favor with her. A few days before our wedding, I was promoted at work even though I was not due for a promotion. That for me was proof of the scripture that he who finds a wife finds a good thing and obtains favor from the Lord (Proverbs 18:22). I pray you will always enjoy favor in your marriage. If you are not married, I pray you will be divinely connected to a spouse.

In spite of the wonderful scriptural provisions and divine promises relating to the matrimonial union, many remain unmarried and some even fear marriage; that is a direct consequence of Satan's war against all good things. Whatever blessing God intends for humanity vexes Satan; it attracts his strongest opposition and resistance. If Satan had his way, there would be no marriage of the sort that pleases God. When he is not busy thwarting or delaying genuinely intended couples, he is packaging calamitous counterfeits and aberrations in the name of marriage for others. Satan wants no one to marry according to divine will and direction. In some cases, his demons proactively attach themselves as spirit spouses to unsuspecting individuals to keep them from marrying whom they should. At times, he afflicts his victims with delusional attitudes that cause them to lose precious time and miss out on fine opportunities to marry. He might cause someone to be too choosy or set unrealistic standards for a spouse.

Friend, marriage is part of your possession. It is your divinely assigned right as a human being and child of God. Even if your claim to that right is compromised by anything you have done or suffered, you are still entitled to reclaim it: "Upon mount Zion there shall be deliverance and holiness, and the house of Israel shall possess their possession" (Obadiah 1:17).

Are you facing an abnormal delay with or hindrance to your marital plans? Have you spoken to God about the problem and obtained divine confirmation that you and your intended are meant for each other? If so, cheerfully stay on course and pursue your plans to fruition. You are about to obtain favor from the Lord, so seek and obtain deliverance from all satanic forces blocking your God-appointed favor. Settle into a life of holiness and you will possess your possession as promised by God. Be expectant. Pray in faith and declare your season of marital favor. Your wedding bells will soon be ringing loud and clear because God knows how to connect you to your life partner. Just be good to everyone God brings your way.

In 2000, I was in Philadelphia looking for a bus to Stroudsburg, PA. I sought directions from a woman, who kindly led me to the bus station when she could have more conveniently shoved a map at me or pointed out the way that I might not have understood. We chatted as we walked; she was pleased to hear that I was a pastor; she asked me for my hotel and phone number.

On my return three days after, she came calling with her prayer request that God would grant her wish to marry and raise a family. We prayed a simple prayer. Barely two weeks later, she called with a testimony of answered prayer. Her college classmate had called her up and proposed marriage, and they are now happily married.

The Prayer Solution

- Be broken every evil power, curse, or covenant delaying my plans for marriage in Jesus's name.
- Every embargo to my marriage be annulled in Jesus's name.
- Father, let your favor of marriage fall on me in Jesus's name.
- Father, connect me to and preserve me for my life partner in Jesus's name.
- Father, show every power or person determined to stop me from getting married that you are the Almighty in Jesus's name.
- (For men): Father, direct my steps to find the bone of my bones in Jesus's name.
- (For women): Father, I position myself to be found by the man whose bone I am in Jesus's name.

Overcoming Marital Storms

Challenges

- When the enemy is working to destabilize your marriage.
- When there are cracks in your marriage that you want mended speedily.
- When there are storms in your marriage and all hopes appear gone.

The Word Solution

Some real-life stories are highly illustrative of God's merciful hand in steadying and preserving shaky marriages.

Story 1

A man left his wife for thirteen years and went to live with another woman. The abandoned wife attended a Holy Spirit service and touched an anointed cloth during Pastor Adeboye's ministration. She went back to her house full of faith, laid her hands on her matrimonial bed, and demanded the return of her husband. A few days after, her husband returned asking for forgiveness.

Story 2

When I was in Ghana in 2012, I learned that a woman there had been sent packing by her husband and the marriage seemed like a lost cause; the man was allegedly having affairs. The woman was drained and exhausted after months of fasting and praying. By the leading of the Holy Spirit, we counseled her to bring God into the matter by unconditionally rendering high praise in the pattern of Jehoshaphat (2 Chronicles 20: 21–22). She started faithfully singing praise to God for an hour every midnight for seven days. In a matter of weeks, her husband came looking for her.

Whatever is happening in your marriage is not beyond God's help. Your spouse may be all the horrible things you fear he or she is, things no one else but you could ever know or guess. A distressed wife said of her husband, "You don't know my husband. He's wicked. He's a miser. He's a drunkard. He's even on drugs. He doesn't love his children. He's a womanizer."

An enraged man had no flattering words about his wife: "You don't know my wife. She's disrespectful. She sleeps around. She doesn't do anything except what her mother tells her to do. She's a bad cook. She's dirty, and our home is unkempt. She never respects me. She never performs her matrimonial duties. She's selfish. And very rude!"

Does any of that describe your spouse a little? What happens when a good product malfunctions? Is it not taken to a technician or to the manufacturer to be fixed? Isn't that why some products have lifetime warranties? Friend, marriage was manufactured by God (Genesis 2:24; Matthew 19:5). He gave out the users' manual too; it stipulates that the product known as marriage must work in specified conditions: wives must reverence their husbands (Ephesians 5:33) and husbands must love their wives (Ephesians 5:28). Are you reading and using that manual for your marriage?

Go back to God if you ignored His manual. He will tell you where you went wrong. He will fix your marriage because it is His product. It is made for you, and it carries a lifetime warranty. Good friend, go to Jesus. He will restore the sweet first love you shared with your spouse.

The Prayer Solution

- Father, speak your peace to every storm in my marriage in Jesus's name.
- Father, teach me how to follow your instructions on marriage in Jesus's name.
- I bind and cast out every stranger in my marriage in Jesus's name.
- I nullify every evil curse against my marriage in Jesus's name.
- Father, reorganize whatever the enemy has disorganized in my marriage in Jesus's name.
- Father, heal, restore, and revive my marriage in Jesus's name.

Overcoming Barrenness

Challenges

- When a wife is slow to conceive or is called barren.
- When miscarriages are frequent occurrences.
- When fruitfulness is a challenge in body, business, or other endeavor.

The Word Solution

Few things can hurt as much as the inability to have a child. Barrenness is a woman's incapacity to conceive and give birth to a child. It is lack of fruitfulness; it is emptiness. It suggests an utter lack of seed to germinate and regenerate. A sown seed is expected to germinate, sprout, become a plant, and produce a harvest; that is nature's principle of increase. God commanded man to multiply and dominate the earth (Genesis 1:22). It is therefore not God's desire or plan for any person or family to be barren.

A certain woman was born again, but like all other wives in that family, she was childless. Her father-in-law was a witch doctor, a situation that put her in direct spiritual warfare. As a born-again Christian, she wised up to God's promise that none of His people would be barren (Deuteronomy 7:9). She was able to claim her rights in Christ through fervent prayer, and to the glory of God, she never again suffered a miscarriage. Today, she has sons and daughters.

God's plan for you as a Christian is that your children will be like olive branches round about your table (Psalm 128:3). God loves increase, and for that reason, He commanded fruitfulness.

Are you fully realizing God's plan for you? Step out in faith today. Trust God and believe His promises. He who made the promise is faithful to fulfill it (Numbers 23:19). Patience is key. God promised Abraham, age seventy-five, a child, and the son of promise, Isaac, was not born until twenty-five years later. That was a lesson in patience. God works with those who trust and obey Him. There is no other way to be happy in Jesus.

Key into the promises of God and wait in trust. Your womb that is called barren will conceive and bear children. The works of your hands will bear fruit of increase. Only believe.

The Prayer Solution

- Every seed of barrenness in my life receive the touch of God and become healed unto fruitfulness as pleasing to God in Jesus's name.
- Father, as I identify with your divine purpose for my life, I reclaim in full the fruitfulness and increase you ordained for me in Jesus's name.
- Father, command fruitfulness into every area of my life in Jesus's name.
- Father, terminate every form of miscarriage or barrenness in my family in Jesus's name.
- Every satanic embargo against my fruitfulness be annulled now in Jesus's name.
- Every curse of barrenness in my ancestral line be broken now in Jesus's name.

Overcoming Miscarriages

Challenges

- When pregnancy fails again and again.
- When businesses crash repeatedly.
- When investment projects become abandoned or die prematurely.

The Word Solution

Miscarriage is the failure to bring a baby to full term. Figuratively speaking, almost every human activity is a type of pregnancy, which is itself a journey. Every uncompleted or abandoned project is a miscarriage. Common examples of miscarriages are academic programs that are not pursued to the end, career paths terminated by disability, penal sanctions, or layoffs, and marriages halted by separation or divorce.

God is never the cause of any form of miscarriage. Jesus gives life; He went about doing good (Acts 10:38) and still does (Matthew 28:20).

Satan is the enemy who goes about like a roaring lion looking for whom to devour (1 Peter 5:8).

You can avoid any form of miscarriage. All it takes is obedience to God's Commandments and precepts. Tithing is one example. God's promise to the tither was that He would not let His vine cast their fruits before time (Malachi 3:11). A sinless life ensures that God's protective hedge around you is never broken for serpent to enter and bite (Ecclesiastes 10:8).

The Bible admonishes us to be sober and vigilant (1 Peter 5:8) as the enemy is on the prowl. Everything you are working for is a pregnancy you have to carefully manage to safe delivery. You need to maintain a prayerful watch over it to prevent a miscarriage. You need to wise up to the ploys of the enemy and be prepared at all times to fight off his predatory incursions.

At the first sign of any threat of a miscarriage, draw up a battle line. A good example is when a pregnant woman has a dream that suggests a miscarriage such as a dream that features blood or an uncompleted journey. Such a dream should be promptly countered with prayers to reverse any curse or enchantment that might have been programmed to trigger a miscarriage. The baby in the womb should be prayed for, blessed, and instructed to harken only to God regarding the right delivery date.

In the same way, you need to deal quickly with any hint of trouble regarding your job, investments, valued relationships, and other interests. An early pushback is an absolute necessity against the devil because silence from you would mean that he has your consent to steal from you.

May God's every miracle reach you, and may you never again suffer any form of miscarriage in Jesus's name.

The Prayer Solution

- Every curse or covenant engendering miscarriages in my life be broken now in Jesus's name.
- I command the completion of every uncompleted project in my life in Jesus's name.

- For ever and ever I reject every form of miscarriage in Jesus's name.
- Every aborted blessing in my life come back to life in Jesus's name.
- Father, silence every force of evil responsible for miscarriage in my life in Jesus's name.

04167804-00967080

Printed in the United States
By Bookmasters